WALT WHITMAN

Leaves of Grass

Selections

Crofts Classics

GENERAL EDITORS

Samuel H. Beer, *Harvard University*

O. B. Hardison, Jr., *The Folger Shakespeare Library*

John Simon

WALT WHITMAN

Leaves of Grass

Selections

EDITED BY

Edwin Haviland Miller

NEW YORK UNIVERSITY

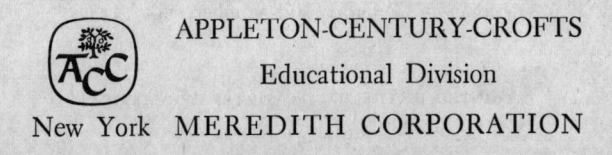

APPLETON-CENTURY-CROFTS
Educational Division
New York MEREDITH CORPORATION

Copyright © 1970 by
MEREDITH CORPORATION
All rights reserved

This book, or parts thereof, must not be used or reproduced in any manner without written permission. For information address the publisher, Appleton-Century-Crofts, Educational Division, Meredith Corporation, 440 Park Avenue South, New York, N.Y. 10016.

659-1

Library of Congress Card Number: 74-91458

PRINTED IN THE UNITED STATES OF AMERICA

390-24190-3

contents

introduction vii

principal dates xi

There Was a Child Went Forth 1

The Sleepers 4

Song of Myself 16

Crossing Brooklyn Ferry 85

As I Ebb'd with the Ocean of Life 93

From Children of Adam 97

    To the Garden the World 97
    From Pent-up Aching Rivers 97
    A Woman Waits for Me 100
    Spontaneous Me 102
    Native Moments 104
    Once I Pass'd through a Populous City 105

From Calamus 106

    In Paths Untrodden 106
    Scented Herbage of My Breast 107
    Long I Thought that Knowledge Alone Would Suffice 109
    Hours Continuing Long, Sore and Heavy-Hearted 110

vi Contents

> Roots and Leaves Themselves Alone 111
> Trickle Drops 112
> I Saw in Louisiana a Live-Oak Growing 112
> We Two Boys Together Clinging 113
> Earth, My Likeness 114
> Here the Frailest Leaves of Me 114

Out of the Cradle Endlessly Rocking 115

From Drum-Taps 122

> Vigil Strange I Kept on the Field One Night 122
> Over the Carnage Rose Prophetic a Voice 123
> By the Bivouac's Fitful Flame 125
> As I Lay with My Head in Your Lap Camerado 125
> Dirge for Two Veterans 126

When Lilacs Last in the Dooryard Bloom'd 128

Passage to India 138

Good-bye My Fancy! 149

Preface *to the 1855 edition of* Leaves of Grass 150

bibliography 173

introduction

American poetry came of age in 1855 when an oversized book with the strange title Leaves of Grass appeared in Brooklyn. The name of the author was not on the title page, but the book was "entered" to "Walter Whitman," printer, journalist, editor, and the author of tales. Although Ralph Waldo Emerson sent a laudatory letter to Whitman a month later, not much attention was paid to the volume in the press. In fact, Whitman himself—anonymously of course—reviewed the book, a practice he pursued throughout most of his career, on the indisputable assumption that the author was the best judge of its contents.

Leaves of Grass was the fourth masterpiece of that remarkable decade in American literature which saw the appearance of The Scarlet Letter in 1850, Moby-Dick in 1851, and Walden in 1854. Clearly the United States was at long last establishing a literature of its own, as Emerson had urged years before, yet only Hawthorne's romance was hailed by critics and the public. The other three books had to struggle for the recognition they clearly deserved.

Whitman did not make matters easy for the public, since he obviously intended Leaves of Grass to be shocking in its unconventionality. The title itself was bewildering to the literal-minded; a daguerreotype pictured a slouching Bohemian with his hat perched precariously on his head, and his underwear showing; a bombastic preface asserted —ironically, in view of the book's reception—"The Americans of all nations at any time upon the earth have probably the fullest poetic nature"; not only were the twelve poems in the slender volume without titles, but also the first poem opened with a brash epic parody, "I celebrate myself"; and several of the poems "undraped" the body in an age which concealed the "limbs" of a piano in pristine yard goods. Those who ventured to read the poetry were troubled by the long lines which were neither metrical in the ordinary sense nor rhymed.

And yet in many respects Whitman was unabashedly American. His egocentricity was not dissimilar from the rugged individualism glorified on the frontier and in the emergent industrial society, and his revolutionary verse and technique should not have alienated a society which seemingly delighted in breaking completely with the past. The difficulty was that despite Whitman's claims, the democratic public was not devoted to poetry. Furthermore, in art this public preferred the old to the new, chaste sentimentality to a vigorous espousal of the body, and solemnity and sobriety to uninhibited playfulness and witty egotism.

At the conclusion of the preface to the first edition of Leaves of Grass Whitman writes, "The proof of a poet is that his country absorbs him as affectionately as he has absorbed it." The truth is that, more than a century later, Whitman has not yet been "absorbed" by the country he loved. He is still more talked about than read—such has been the price of the personality cult he encouraged—or he is praised for his least original creations. Only recently, for example, has the extraordinary dream landscape revealed in "The Sleepers" received adequate recognition for its acute psychological perceptions. Many of his American successors have made "A Pact" with him as reluctantly as Ezra Pound does in his well-known poem, perhaps because there is something about Whitman that arouses either adulation that borders on fanaticism or contempt that almost hysterically denies him any merits at all.

Probably Whitman's poetry will always be difficult. Despite the apparent simplicity of his language and symbols, exegesis is not easy. Whitman is elusive—sometimes deliberately—and he is so childlike in his undifferentiated acceptance of nature and people that he offends our reason and our smug distinctions. Although he likes to proclaim himself a democratic bard and sometimes indulges in embarrassingly patriotic rhetoric, his greatest poems are not narrowly chauvinistic: his universal and timeless landscape is the habitation of Everyman. American as Whitman is, the patriotic reading is the least rewarding of critical approaches. Although idolators have sometimes almost deified Whitman and have made Leaves of Grass into a modern Bible, their understandable but misguided zeal should not obscure the fact that the poet himself frequently termed his poetry religious, and that Swinburne and others were reminded of Blake's mystical verse. Since Whitman's seeming mysticism is not, at least superficially, traditional, one critic, James E. Miller, Jr., has characterized it as "inverted mysticism," and Malcolm Cowley and more recently V. K. Chari have found parallels with Oriental thought. It is perhaps not implausible to regard Whitman's "vision" as an anticipation of the hedonistic secularism of Henry Miller. Or one may see Whitman's poetry, like Walden, as a commentary upon the dehumanization and desperateness of man's life in the Age of the Dynamo. Or Leaves of Grass may be read as a portrait of the artist, as complex and astute as James Joyce's study in his famous novel. Or, finally, Whitman may be read as an analyst who, like Freud, came to an understanding of reality through a courageous journey into the depths of his own personality.

One does not have to seek for a meaning or even the meaning of these poems. Whitman does not ask the reader to live according to his amorphous tenets; in fact, he observes, quite sincerely, "He most honors my style who learns under it to destroy the teacher." One can enjoy his bravado, his wit, his animal spirits, and his gaiety. The gusto and energy of "Song of Myself" are sheer delight. On the other hand, his detractors notwithstanding, Whitman does not close his eyes to evil or misery; one has only to look at "The Sleepers" or "Song of Myself" to appreciate this. The "Calamus" poems, Whitman's chants of love, are filled not only with tenderness but also with a loneliness that sometimes is almost overwhelming. Although he kept his faith in democratic man and democracy, he no more deluded himself as to the nature of reality than did Hawthorne or Melville. But, like Emerson and Thoreau, he disdained to despair of the only life man can ever know: the bewildering, chaotic, but exciting present. And so he sings of "happiness." For Leaves of Grass is, like Don Quixote, one of the saddest and happiest books ever written.

x   introduction

a note on the text

Whitman revised his poetry throughout his life, and in the last edition of Leaves of Grass requested that his final text be used in subsequent printings. However, with a few exceptions—the most notable being "Out of the Cradle Endlessly Rocking"—I have used the earliest versions of the poems, on the simple, though admittedly debatable, premise that the original impulse that gave rise to a poem is more faithfully rendered in the earliest version than in later revisions. The complete text of the preface to the 1855 edition of Leaves of Grass is given as an appendix.

E. H. M.

principal dates in the life of Walt Whitman

1819	Born on May 31 at West Hills, near Huntington, Long Island.
1830–34	Learns printing trade.
1836–38	Teaches school at various places on Long Island.
1838–39	Edits *The Long Islander*, a weekly newspaper.
1840–41	Again teaches school. Begins to publish tales in the *Democratic Review*.
1842	Edits a daily newspaper in New York City, the *Aurora*.
1846–48	Edits the Brooklyn *Daily Eagle*.
1848	Travels to New Orleans to work for the *Crescent*. Returns to Brooklyn in June and edits the Brooklyn *Freeman*.
1855	*Leaves of Grass*, first edition. Emerson greets the new poet in a famous letter on July 21.
1856	*Leaves of Grass*, second edition, with Emerson's letter and Whitman's reply.
1857–59	Edits the Brooklyn *Times*.
1860	*Leaves of Grass*, third edition, the first commercial publication of his poetry.
1862–65	A frequent visitor in Washington military hospitals.
1865	Appointed, in January, a clerk in the Department of the Interior, discharged on June 30, and employed in the Attorney General's Office on the following day. *Drum-Taps* appears in May, and *Drum-Taps and Sequel*, which cludes "When Lilacs Last in the Dooryard Bloom'd," issued in the fall.

xii principal dates

1866	William D. O'Connor, Whitman's friend, publishes *The Good Gray Poet*.
1867	*Leaves of Grass*, fourth edition.
1868	*Poems of Walt Whitman*, selected and expurgated (with the poet's consent) by William Michael Rossetti, appears in England.
1871–72	*Leaves of Grass*, fifth edition, *Democratic Vistas*, and *Passage to India*.
1873	Whitman suffers a paralytic stroke on January 23, later returns to Camden, where he lives with his brother, George Washington Whitman, until 1884.
1876	*Leaves of Grass*, sixth edition, the so-called Centennial Edition.
1879	Gives first public lecture in New York on "The Death of Abraham Lincoln," which he is to repeat many times during the next decade.
1881–82	*Leaves of Grass*, seventh edition, printed in Boston by James R. Osgood. The District Attorney threatens legal action unless certain poems and lines are removed. Publication is resumed in June, 1882, by Rees Welsh in Philadelphia.
1882	*Specimen Days and Collect*, Whitman's prose miscellany.
1883	Richard Maurice Bucke publishes *Walt Whitman*; carefully edited by Whitman, it is the fullest biographical study printed in the poet's lifetime.
1884	Moves into his own "shanty" on Mickle Street, Camden, where he continues until his death to receive visitors from all over the world.
1887	Thomas Eakins paints Whitman's portait.
1888	*Leaves of Grass*, eighth edition, also *November Boughs*.
1891	*Leaves of Grass*, ninth edition, the "death-bed" edition, also *Good-Bye My Fancy*.
1892	Dies on March 26, and is buried in a vault he designed in Harleigh Cemetery, Camden.

There Was a Child Went Forth

There was a child went forth every day,
And the first object he looked upon and received with
 wonder or pity or love or dread, that object he
 became,
And that object became part of him for the day or a
 certain part of the day . . . . or for many years or
 stretching cycles of years.

The early lilacs became part of this child,
And grass, and white and red morningglories, and white
 and red clover, and the song of the phœbe-bird,
And the March-born lambs, and the sow's pink-faint
 litter, and the mare's foal, and the cow's calf, and the
 noisy brood of the barnyard or by the mire of the
 pondside . . and the fish suspending themselves so
 curiously below there . . and the beautiful curious
 liquid . . and the water-plants with their graceful
 flat heads . . all became part of him.

And the field-sprouts of April and May became part of
 him . . . . wintergrain sprouts, and those of the
 light-yellow corn, and of the esculent roots of the
 garden,
And the appletrees covered with blossoms, and the fruit
 afterward . . . . and woodberries . . and the
 commonest weeds by the road;
And the old drunkard staggering home from the outhouse
 of the tavern whence he had lately risen,
And the schoolmistress that passed on her way to the
 school . . and the friendly boys that passed . . and
 the quarrelsome boys . . and the tidy and freshcheeked
 girls . . and the barefoot negro boy and girl,
And all the changes of city and country wherever
 he went.

2 Walt Whitman

His own parents . . he that had propelled the fatherstuff
   at night, and fathered him . . and she that conceived
   him in her womb and birthed him . . . . they
   gave this child more of themselves than that,
They gave him afterward every day . . . . they and of
   them became part of him.

The mother at home quietly placing the dishes on the
   suppertable,
The mother with mild words . . . . clean her cap
   and gown . . . . a wholesome odor falling off her
   person and clothes as she walks by:
The father, strong, selfsufficient, manly, mean, angered,
   unjust,
The blow, the quick loud word, the tight bargain, the
   crafty lure,
The family usages, the language, the company, the
   furniture . . . . the yearning and swelling heart,
Affection that will not be gainsayed . . . . The sense of
   what is real . . . . the thought if after all it should
   prove unreal,
The doubts of daytime and the doubts of nighttime
   . . . the curious whether and how,
Whether that which appears so is so . . . . Or is it all
   flashes and specks?
Men and women crowding fast in the streets . . if
   they are not flashes and specks what are they?
The streets themselves, and the facades of houses
   . . . . the goods in the windows,
Vehicles . . teams . . the tiered wharves, and the
   huge crossing at the ferries;
The village on the highland seen from afar at sunset
   . . . . the river between,
Shadows . . aureola and mist . . light falling on
   roofs and gables of white or brown, three miles off,
The schooner near by sleepily dropping down the tide
   . . the little boat slacktowed astern,
The hurrying tumbling waves and quickbroken crests
   and slapping;
The strata of colored clouds . . . . the long bar of
   maroontint away solitary by itself . . . . the spread
   of purity it lies motionless in,

There Was a Child Went Forth

The horizon's edge, the flying seacrow, the fragrance of
    saltmarsh and shoremud;   30
These became part of that child who went forth every
    day, and who now goes and will always go forth
    every day,
And these become of him or her that peruses them now.

expres well his early life

The Sleepers

[1] I wander all night in my vision,
  Stepping with light feet . . . . swiftly and noiselessly stepping and stopping,
  Bending with open eyes over the shut eyes of sleepers;
  Wandering and confused . . . . lost to myself . . . . ill-assorted . . . . contradictory,
  Pausing and gazing and bending and stopping.

  How solemn they look there, stretched and still;
  How quiet they breathe, the little children in their cradles.

  The wretched features of ennuyees, the white features of corpses, the livid faces of drunkards, the sick-gray faces of onanists,
  The gashed bodies on battlefields, the insane in their strong-doored rooms, the sacred idiots,
  The newborn emerging from gates and the dying emerging from gates,
  The night pervades them and enfolds them.

  The married couple sleep calmly in their bed, he with his palm on the hip of the wife, and she with her palm on the hip of the husband,
  The sisters sleep lovingly side by side in their bed,
  The men sleep lovingly side by side in theirs,
  And the mother sleeps with her little child carefully wrapped.

This poem was titled "Night Poem" in 1856, "Sleep-Chasings" in 1860, and finally "The Sleepers" in 1871. In 1881 two major excisions were made: ll. 60–70 and 127–134. The final two lines of the poem were deleted in 1856 8 **ennuyees** bored or annoyed people

The blind sleep, and the deaf and dumb sleep,
The prisoner sleeps well in the prison . . . . the runaway son sleeps,
The murderer that is to be hung next day . . . . how does he sleep?
And the murdered person . . . . how does he sleep?

The female that loves unrequited sleeps, 20
And the male that loves unrequited sleeps;
The head of the moneymaker that plotted all day sleeps,
And the enraged and treacherous dispositions sleep.

I stand with drooping eyes by the worstsuffering and restless,
I pass my hands soothingly to and fro a few inches from them;
The restless sink in their beds . . . . they fitfully sleep.

The earth recedes from me into the night,
I saw that it was beautiful . . . . and I see that what is not the earth is beautiful.

I go from bedside to bedside . . . . I sleep close with the other sleepers, each in turn;
I dream in my dream all the dreams of the other dreamers, 30
And I become the other dreamers.

I am a dance . . . . Play up there! the fit is whirling me fast.

I am the everlaughing . . . . it is new moon and twilight,
I see the hiding of douceurs . . . . I see nimble ghosts whichever way I look,
Cache and cache again deep in the ground and sea, and where it is neither ground or sea.

34 **douceurs** delights or sweets (French)

Well do they do their jobs, those journeymen divine,
Only from me can they hide nothing and would not if
    they could;
I reckon I am their boss, and they make me a pet besides,
And surround me, and lead me and run ahead when I
    walk,
And lift their cunning covers and signify me with
    stretched arms, and resume the way;   40
Onward we move, a gay gang of blackguards with
    mirthshouting music and wildflapping pennants of joy.

I am the actor and the actress . . . . the voter . . the
    politician,
The emigrant and the exile . . the criminal that stood
    in the box,
He who has been famous, and he who shall be famous
    after today,
The stammerer . . . . the wellformed person . . the
    wasted or feeble person.

I am she who adorned herself and folded her hair
    expectantly,
My truant lover has come and it is dark.

Double yourself and receive me darkness,
Receive me and my lover too . . . . he will not let me
    go without him.

I roll myself upon you as upon a bed . . . . I resign
    myself to the dusk.   50

He whom I call answers me and takes the place of my
    lover,
He rises with me silently from the bed.

Darkness you are gentler than my lover . . . . his
    flesh was sweaty and panting,
I feel the hot moisture yet that he left me.

My hands are spread forth . . I pass them in all
    directions,
I would sound up the shadowy shore to which you are
    journeying.

The Sleepers   7

Be careful, darkness . . . . already, what was it touched me?
I thought my lover had gone . . . . else darkness and he are one,
I hear the heart-beat . . . . I follow . . I fade away.

O hotcheeked and blushing! O foolish hectic!   60
O for pity's sake, no one must see me now! . . . . my clothes were stolen while I was abed,
Now I am thrust forth, where shall I run?

Pier that I saw dimly last night when I looked from the windows,
Pier out from the main, let me catch myself with you and stay . . . . I will not chafe you;
I feel ashamed to go naked about the world,
And am curious to know where my feet stand . . . . and what is this flooding me, childhood or manhood . . . . and the hunger that crossses the bridge between.

The cloth laps a first sweet eating and drinking,
Laps life-swelling yolks . . . . laps ear of rose-corn, milky and just ripened:
The white teeth stay, and the boss-tooth advances in darkness,
And liquor is spilled on lips and bosoms by touching glasses, and the best liquor afterward.   70

[2] I descend my western course . . . . my sinews are flaccid,
Perfume and youth course through me, and I am their wake.

It is my face yellow and wrinkled instead of the old woman's,
I sit low in a strawbottom chair and carefully darn my grandson's stockings.

8   Walt Whitman

It is I too . . . . the sleepless widow looking out on the winter midnight,
I see the sparkles of starshine on the icy and pallid earth.

A shroud I see—and I am the shroud . . . . I wrap a body and lie in the coffin;
It is dark here underground . . . . it is not evil or pain here . . . . it is blank here, for reasons.

It seems to me that everything in the light and air ought to be happy;
Whoever is not in his coffin and the dark grave, let him know he has enough.   80

[3]   I see a beautiful gigantic swimmer swimming naked through the eddies of the sea,
His brown hair lies close and even to his head . . . . he strikes out with courageous arms . . . . he urges himself with his legs.

I see his white body . . . . I see his undaunted eyes;
I hate the swift-running eddies that would dash him headforemost on the rocks.

What are you doing you ruffianly red-trickled waves?
Will you kill the courageous giant? Will you kill him in the prime of his middle age?

Steady and long he struggles;
He is baffled and banged and bruised . . . . he holds out while his strength holds out,
The slapping eddies are spotted with his blood . . . . they bear him away . . . . they roll him and swing him and turn him:
His beautiful body is borne in the circling eddies . . . . it is continually bruised on rocks,   90
Swiftly and out of sight is borne the brave corpse.

The Sleepers 9

[4] I turn but do not extricate myself;
Confused .... a pastreading .... another, but with darkness yet.

The beach is cut by the razory ice-wind .... the wreck-guns sound,
The tempest lulls and the moon comes floundering through the drifts.

I look where the ship helplessly heads end on .... I hear the burst as she strikes . . I head the howls of dismay .... they grow fainter and fainter.

I cannot aid with my wringing fingers;
I can but rush to the surf and let it drench me and freeze upon me.
I search with the crowd .... not one of the company is washed to us alive;
In the morning I help pick up the dead and lay them in rows in a barn.   100

[5] Now of the old war-days . . the defeat of Brooklyn;
Washington stands inside the lines . . he stands on the entrenched hills amid a crowd of officers,
His face is cold and damp .... he cannot repress the weeping drops .... he lifts the glass perpetually to his eyes .... the color is blanched from his cheeks,
He sees the slaughter of the southern braves confided to him by their parents.

The same at last and at last when peace is declared,
He stands in the room of the old tavern .... the wellbeloved soldiers all pass through.

The officers speechless and slow draw near in their turns,
The chief encircles their necks with his arm and kisses them on the cheek,

101 **defeat of Brooklyn** the Battle of Brooklyn Heights on August 27, 1776

He kisses lightly the wet cheeks one after another . . . .
he shakes hands and bids goodbye to the army.

[6] Now I tell what my mother told me today as we sat at
dinner together,
Of when she was a nearly grown girl living home with her
parents on the old homestead.

A red squaw came one breakfastime to the old
homestead,
On her back she carried a bundle of rushes for
rushbottoming chairs;
Her hair straight shiny coarse black and profuse
halfenveloped her face,
Her step was free and elastic . . . . her voice sounded
exquisitely as she spoke.

My mother looked in delight and amazement at the
stranger,
She looked at the beauty of her tallborne face and full and
pliant limbs,
The more she looked upon her she loved her,
Never before had she seen such wonderful beauty and
purity;
She made her sit on a bench by the jamb of the fireplace
. . . . she cooked food for her,
She had no work to give her but she gave her
remembrance and fondness.

The red squaw staid all the forenoon, and toward the
middle of the afternoon she went away;
O my mother was loth to have her go away,
All the week she thought of her . . . . she watched for
her many a month,
She remembered her many a winter and many a summer,
But the red squaw never came nor was heard of there
again.

123 **loth** variant of loath

The Sleepers 11

Now Lucifer was not dead . . . . or if he was I am his
  sorrowful terrible heir;
I have been wronged . . . . I am oppressed I
  hate him that oppresses me,
I will either destroy him, or he shall release him.

Damn him! how he does defile me, 130
How he informs against my brother and sister and takes
  pay for their blood,
How he laughs when I look down the bend after the
  steamboat that carries away my woman.

Now the vast dusk bulk that is the whale's bulk . . . .
  it seems mine,
Warily, sportsman! though I lie so sleepy and sluggish,
  my tap is death.

[7] A show of the summer softness . . . . a contact of some-
  thing unseen . . . . an amour of the light and air;
I am jealous and overwhelmed with friendliness,
And will go gallivant with the light and the air myself,
And have an unseen something to be in contact with
  them also.

O love and summer! you are in the dreams and in me,
Autumn and winter are in the dreams . . . . the
  farmer goes with his thrift,
140
The droves and crops increase . . . . the barns are
  wellfilled.

Elements merge in the night . . . . ships make tacks in
  the dreams . . . . the sailor sails . . . . the exile
  returns home,
The fugitive returns unharmed . . . . the immigrant is
  back beyond months and years;
The poor Irishman lives in the simple house of his
  childhood, with the wellknown neighbors and faces,
They warmly welcome him . . . . he is barefoot again
  . . . . he forgets he is welloff;

The Dutchman voyages home, and the Scotchman and
   Welchman voyage home . . and the native of the
   Mediterranean voyages home;
To every port of England and France and Spain enter
   wellfilled ships;
The Swiss foots it toward his hills . . . . the Prussian
   goes his way, and the Hungarian his way, and the Pole
   goes his way,
The Swede returns, and the Dane and Norwegian return.

The homeward bound and the outward bound,   150
The beautiful lost swimmer, the ennuyee, the onanist,
   the female that loves unrequited, the moneymaker,
The actor and actress . . those through with their parts
   and those waiting to commence,
The affectionate boy, the husband and wife, the voter, the
   nominee that is chosen and the nominee that has failed,
The great already known, and the great anytime after
   to-day,
The stammerer, the sick, the perfectformed, the homely,
The criminal that stood in the box, the judge that sat
   and sentenced him, the fluent lawyers, the jury, the
   audience,
The laugher and weeper, the dancer, the midnight
   widow, the red squaw,
The consumptive, the erysipalite, the idiot, he that is
   wronged,
The antipodes, and every one between this and them in
   the dark,
I swear they are averaged now . . . . one is no better
   than the other,   160
The night and sleep have likened them and restored
   them.

I swear they are all beautiful,
Every one that sleeps is beautiful . . . . every thing in
   the dim night is beautiful,
The wildest and bloodiest is over and all is peace.

158 **erysipalite** from *erysipelas*, an acute febrile disease with
intense inflammation of the skin, usually about the hands

The Sleepers 13

Peace is always beautiful,
The myth of heaven indicates peace and night.

The myth of heaven indicates the soul;
The soul is always beautiful .... it appears more or it
    appears less .... it comes or lags behind,
It comes from its embowered garden and looks pleasantly
    on itself and encloses the world;
Perfect and clean the genitals previously jetting, and
    perfect and clean the womb cohering,   170
The head wellgrown and proportioned and plumb, and
    the bowels and joints proportioned and plumb.

The soul is always beautiful,
The universe is duly in order .... every thing is in its
    place,
What is arrived is in its place, and what waits is in its
    place;
The twisted skull waits .... the watery or rotten blood
    waits,
The child of the glutton or venerealee waits long, and the
    child of the drunkard waits long, and the drunkard
    himself waits long,
The sleepers that lived and died wait .... the far
    advanced are to go on in their turns, and the far
    behind are to go on in their turns,
The diverse shall be no less diverse, but they shall flow
    and unite .... they unite now.

[8] The sleepers are very beautiful as they lie unclothed,
    They flow hand in hand over the whole earth from east
        to west as they lie unclothed;   180
    The Asiatic and African are hand in hand .. the
        European and American are hand in hand,
    Learned and unlearned are hand in hand .. and male
        and female are hand in hand;
    The bare arm of the girl crosses the bare breast of her
        lover .... they press close without lust ....
        his lips press her neck,

The father holds his grown or ungrown son in his arms
with measureless love . . . . and the son holds the
father in his arms with measureless love,
The white hair of the mother shines on the white
wrist of the daughter,
The breath of the boy goes with the breath of the man
. . . . friend is inarmed by friend,
The scholar kisses the teacher and the teacher kisses the
scholar . . . . the wronged is made right,
The call of the slave is one with the master's call . .
and the master salutes the slave,
The felon steps forth from the prison . . . . the insane
becomes sane . . . . the suffering of sick persons is
relieved,
The sweatings and fevers stop . . the throat that was
unsound is sound . . the lungs of the consumptive
are resumed . . the poor distressed head is free,   190
The joints of the rheumatic move as smoothly as ever,
and smoother than ever,
Stiflings and passages open . . . . the paralysed become
supple,
The swelled and convulsed and congested awake to
themselves in condition,
They pass the invigoration of the night and the
chemistry of the night and awake.

I too pass from the night;
I stay awhile away O night, but I return to you again
and love you;
Why should I be afraid to trust myself to you?
I am not afraid . . . . I have been well brought
forward by you;
I love the rich running day, but I do not desert her in
whom I lay so long:
I know not how I came of you, and I know not where I
go with you . . . . but I know I came well and shall
go well.   200

I will stop only a time with the night . . . . and rise
betimes.

I will duly pass the day O my mother and duly return
  to you;
Not you will yield forth the dawn again more surely
  than you will yield forth me again,
Not the womb yields the babe in its time more surely
  than I shall be yielded from you in my time.

forms of science — science is something special

Science — essence in put to transcend, to creates forms according to life rather than according to form

Song of Myself

[1] I celebrate myself,
And what I assume you shall assume,
For every atom belonging to me as good belongs to you.

I loafe and invite my soul,
I lean and loafe at my ease . . . . observing a spear of summer grass.

[2] Houses and rooms are full of perfumes . . . . the shelves are crowded with perfumes,
I breathe the fragrance myself, and know it and like it,
The distillation would intoxicate me also, but I shall not let it.

The atmosphere is not a perfume . . . . it has no taste of the distillation . . . . it is odorless,
It is for my mouth forever . . . . I am in love with it,
I will go to the bank by the wood and become undisguised and naked,
I am mad for it to be in contact with me.

The smoke of my own breath,
Echoes, ripples, and buzzed whispers . . . . loveroot, silkthread, crotch and vine,
My respiration and inspiration . . . . the beating of my heart . . . . the passing of blood and air through my lungs,
The sniff of green leaves and dry leaves, and of the shore and darkcolored sea-rocks, and of hay in the barn,
The sound of the belched words of my voice . . . . words loosed to the eddies of the wind,

Untitled in 1855; "Poem of Walt Whitman, an American" in 1856; "Walt Whitman" in 1860; present title in 1881

I & you combined because we all stem from the same nation all of the country & people

Song of Myself   17

A few light kisses . . . . a few embraces . . . . a
  reaching around of arms,
The play of shine and shade on the trees as the supple
  boughs wag,
The delight alone or in the rush of the streets, or along
  the fields and hillsides,   20
The feeling of health . . . . the full-noon trill . . . .
  the song of me rising from bed and meeting the sun.

Have you reckoned a thousand acres much? Have you
  reckoned the earth much?
Have you practiced so long to learn to read?
Have you felt so proud to get at the meaning of poems?

Stop this day and night with me and you shall possess
  the origin of all poems,
You shall possess the good of the earth and sun . . . .
  there are millions of suns left,
You shall no longer take things at second or third
  hand . . . . nor look through the eyes of the dead
  . . . . nor feed on spectres in books,
You shall not look through my eyes either, nor take
  things from me,
You shall listen to all sides and filter them from yourself.

[3] I have heard what the talkers were talking . . . . the
  talk of the beginning and the end,   30
But I do not talk of the beginning or the end.

There was never any more inception than there is now,
Nor any more youth or age than there is now;
And will never be any more perfection than there is now,
Nor any more heaven or hell than there is now.

Urge and urge and urge,
Always the procreant urge of the world.

Out of the dimness opposite equals advance . . . .
  Always substance and increase,
Always a knit of identity . . . . always distinction
  . . . . always a breed of life.

To elaborate is no avail . . . . Learned and unlearned
  feel that it is so.   40

Sure as the most certain sure . . . . plumb in the
  uprights, well entretied, braced in the beams,
Stout as a horse, affectionate, haughty, electrical,
I and this mystery here we stand.

Clear and sweet is my soul . . . . and clear and sweet
  is all that is not my soul.

Lack one lacks both . . . . and the unseen is proved
  by the seen,
Till that becomes unseen and receives proof in its turn.

Showing the best and dividing it from the worst, age
  vexes age,
Knowing the perfect fitness and equanimity of things,
  while they discuss I am silent, and go bathe and
  admire myself.

Welcome is every organ and attribute of me, and of
  any man hearty and clean,
Not an inch nor a particle of an inch is vile, and none
  shall be less familiar than the rest.   50

I am satisfied . . . . I see, dance, laugh, sing;
As God comes a loving bedfellow and sleeps at my
  side all night and close on the peep of the day,
And leaves for me baskets covered with white towels
  bulging the house with their plenty,
Shall I postpone my acceptation and realization and
  scream at my eyes,
That they turn from gazing after and down the road,
And forthwith cipher and show me to a cent,
Exactly the contents of one, and exactly the contents
  of two, and which is ahead?

41 **entretied** "cross-braced," a carpenter's term

Song of Myself 19

[4] Trippers and askers surround me,
People I meet . . . . the effect upon me of my
 early life . . . . of the ward and city I live in
 . . . . of the nation,
The latest news . . . . discoveries, inventions,
 societies . . . . authors old and new,
My dinner, dress, associates, looks, business, compliments,
 dues,
The real or fancied indifference of some man or
 woman I love,
The sickness of one of my folks—or of myself . . . .
 or ill-doing . . . . or loss or lack of money . . . .
 or depressions or exaltations,
They come to me days and nights and go from me again,
But they are not Me myself.

Apart from the pulling and hauling stands what I am,
Stands amused, complacent, compassionating, idle,
 unitary,
Looks down, is erect, bends an arm on an impalpable
 certain rest,
Looks with its sidecurved head curious what will come
 next,
Both in and out of the game, and watching and
 wondering at it.

Backward I see in my own days where I sweated
 through fog with linguists and contenders,
I have no mockings or arguments . . . . I witness
 and wait.

[5] I believe in you my soul . . . . the other I am must
 not abase itself to you,
And you must not be abased to the other.

Loafe with me on the grass . . . . loose the stop
 from your throat,
Not words, not music or rhyme I want . . . . not
 custom or lecture, not even the best,
Only the lull I like, the hum of your valved voice.

20 Walt Whitman

I mind how we lay in June, such a transparent
   summer morning;
You settled your head athwart my hips and gently
   turned over upon me,
And parted the shirt from my bosom-bone, and
   plunged your tongue to my barestript heart,   80
And reached till you felt my beard, and reached till
   you held my feet.

Swiftly arose and spread around me the peace and joy
   and knowledge that pass all the art and argument
   of the earth;
And I know that the hand of God is the elderhand
   of my own,
And I know that the spirit of God is the eldest brother
   of my own,
And that all the men ever born are also my brothers
   . . . . and the women my sisters and lovers,
And that a kelson of the creation is love;
And limitless are leaves stiff or drooping in the fields,
And brown ants in the little wells beneath them,
And mossy scabs of the wormfence, and heaped stones,
   and elder and mullen and pokeweed.

[6] A child said, What is the grass? fetching it to me with
        full hands;   90
     How could I answer the child? . . . . I do not know
        what it is any more than he.

I guess it must be the flag of my disposition, out of
   hopeful green stuff woven.

86 **kelson** variant of keelson, "a structure of timbers in a wooden ship parallel with and above the keel and fastened to it by long bolts passing through the floor timbers"

Song of Myself 21

Or I guess it is the handkerchief of the Lord,
A scented gift and remembrancer designedly dropped,
Bearing the owner's name someway in the corners,
  that we may see and remark, and say Whose?

Or I guess the grass is itself a child . . . . the produced
  babe of the vegetation.

Or I guess it is a uniform hieroglyphic,
And it means, Sprouting alike in broad zones and
  narrow zones,
Growing among black folks as among white,
Kanuck, Tuckahoe, Congressman, Cuff, I give them
  the same, I receive them the same.   100

And now it seems to me the beautiful uncut hair of
  graves.

Tenderly will I use you curling grass,
It may be you transpire from the breasts of young men,
It may be if I had known them I would have loved
  them;
It may be you are from old people and from women,
  and from offspring taken soon out of their mothers'
  laps,
And here you are the mothers' laps.

This grass is very dark to be from the white heads of
  old mothers,
Darker than the colorless beards of old men,
Dark to come from under the faint red roofs of mouths.

O I perceive after all so many uttering tongues!   110
And I perceive they do not come from the roofs of
  mouths for nothing.

100 **Kanuck** French Canadian   **Tuckahoe** Virginian living east
of the Blue Ridge Mountains   **Cuff** a Negro

22 Walt Whitman

I wish I could translate the hints about the dead young
  men and women,
And the hints about old men and mothers, and the
  offspring taken soon out of their laps.

What do you think has become of the young and
  old men?
And what do you think has become of the women
  and children?

They are alive and well somewhere;
The smallest sprout shows there is really no death,
And if ever there was it led forward life, and does not
  wait at the end to arrest it,
And ceased the moment life appeared.

All goes onward and outward . . . . and nothing
  collapses,
And to die is different from what any one supposed,
  and luckier.

[7] Has any one supposed it lucky to be born?
I hasten to inform him or her it is just as lucky to die,
  and I know it.

I pass death with the dying, and birth with the
  new-washed babe . . . . and am not contained
  between my hat and boots,
And peruse manifold objects, no two alike, and every
  one good,
The earth good, and the stars good, and their adjuncts
  all good.

I am not an earth nor an adjunct of an earth,
I am the mate and companion of people, all just as
  immortal and fathomless as myself;
They do not know how immortal, but I know.

Every kind for itself and its own . . . . for me mine
  male and female,

For me all that have been boys and that love women,
For me the man that is proud and feels how it stings to be slighted,
For me the sweetheart and the old maid . . . . for me mothers and the mothers of mothers,
For me lips that have smiled, eyes that have shed tears,
For me children and the begetters of children.

Who need be afraid of the merge?
Undrape . . . . you are not guilty to me, nor stale nor discarded,
I see through the broadcloth and gingham whether or no,
And am around, tenacious, acquisitive, tireless . . . . and can never be shaken away.

[8] The little one sleeps in its cradle,
I lift the gauze and look a long time, and silently brush away flies with my hand.

The youngster and the redfaced girl turn aside up the bushy hill,
I peeringly view them from the top.

The suicide sprawls on the bloody floor of the bedroom,
It is so . . . . I witnessed the corpse . . . . there the pistol had fallen.

The blab of the pave . . . . the tires of carts and sluff of bootsoles and talk of the promenaders,
The heavy omnibus, the driver with his interrogating thumb, the clank of the shod horses on the granite floor,
The carnival of sleighs, the clinking and shouted jokes and pelts of snowballs;
The hurrahs for popular favorites . . . . the fury of roused mobs,
The flap of the curtained litter—the sick man inside, borne to the hospital,

24   Walt Whitman

The meeting of enemies, the sudden oath, the blows
   and fall,
The excited crowd—the policeman with his star
   quickly working his passage to the centre of the
   crowd;
The impressive stones that receive and return so
   many echoes,
The souls moving along . . . . are they invisible
   while the least atom of the stones is visible?
What groans of overfed or half-starved who fall on
   the flags sunstruck or in fits,
What exclamations of women taken suddenly, who
   hurry home and give birth to babes,
What living and buried speech is always vibrating
   here . . . . what howls restrained by decorum,
Arrests of criminals, slights, adulterous offers made,
   acceptances, rejections with convex lips,
I mind them or the resonance of them . . . . I come
   again and again.

[9] The big doors of the country-barn stand open and
      ready,   160
    The dried grass of the harvest-time loads the
      slow-drawn wagon,
    The clear light plays on the brown gray and green
      intertinged,
    The armfuls are packed to the sagging mow:
    I am there . . . . I help . . . . I came stretched
      atop of the load,
    I felt its soft jolts . . . . one leg reclined on the
      other,
    I jump from the crossbeams, and seize the clover and
      timothy,
    And roll head over heels, and tangle my hair full of
      wisps.

[10] Alone far in the wilds and mountains I hunt,
     Wandering amazed at my own lightness and glee,
     In the late afternoon choosing a safe spot to pass the
       night,   170

Song of Myself   25

Kindling a fire and broiling the freshkilled game,
Soundly falling asleep on the gathered leaves, my dog
 and gun by my side.

The Yankee clipper is under her three skysails . . . .
 she cuts the sparkle and scud,
My eyes settle the land . . . . I bend at her prow
 or shout joyously from the deck.

The boatmen and clamdiggers arose early and stopped
 for me,
I tucked my trowser-ends in my boots and went and
 had a good time,
You should have been with us that day round the
 chowder-kettle.

I saw the marriage of the trapper in the open air in
 the far-west . . . . the bride was a red girl,
Her father and his friends sat near by crosslegged and
 dumbly smoking . . . . they had moccasins to
 their feet and large thick blankets hanging from
 their shoulders;
On a bank lounged the trapper . . . . he was dressed
 mostly in skins . . . . his luxuriant beard and
 curls protected his neck,
One hand rested on his rifle . . . . the other hand
 held firmly the wrist of the red girl,
She had long eyelashes . . . . her head was bare
 . . . . her coarse straight locks descended upon
 her voluptuous limbs and reached to her feet.

The runaway slave came to my house and stopped
 outside,
I heard his motions crackling the twigs of the
 woodpile,
Through the swung half-door of the kitchen I saw
 him limpsey and weak,
And went where he sat on a log, and led him in and
 assured him,

173 **scud** ocean spray or loose vapory clouds   185 **limpsey** limp
from exhaustion

26   *Walt Whitman*

And brought water and filled a tub for his sweated
   body and bruised feet,
And gave him a room that entered from my own, and
   gave him some coarse clean clothes,
And remember perfectly well his revolving eyes and
   his awkwardness,
And remember putting plasters on the galls of his
   neck and ankles;   190
He staid with me a week before he was recuperated
   and passed north,
I had him sit next me at table . . . . my firelock
   leaned in the corner.

[11] Twenty-eight young men bathe by the shore,
Twenty-eight young men, and all so friendly,
Twenty-eight years of womanly life, and all so
   lonesome.

She owns the fine house by the rise of the bank,
She hides handsome and richly drest aft the blinds of
   the window.

Which of the young men does she like the best?
Ah the homeliest of them is beautiful to her.

Where are you off to, lady? for I see you,   200
You splash in the water there, yet stay stock still in
   your room.

Dancing and laughing along the beach came the
   twenty-ninth bather,
The rest did not see her, but she saw them and loved
   them.

The beards of the young men glistened with wet, it
   ran from their long hair,
Little streams passed all over their bodies.

---

193 **Twenty-eight** possibly the lunar cycle or the menstrual period

An unseen hand also passed over their bodies,
It descended tremblingly from their temples and ribs.

The young men float on their backs, their white
   bellies swell to the sun . . . . they do not ask who
   seizes fast to them,
They do not know who puffs and declines with
   pendant and bending arch,
They do not think whom they souse with spray.   210

[12] The butcher-boy puts off his killing-clothes, or
   sharpens his knife at the stall in the market,
I loiter enjoying his repartee and his shuffle and
   breakdown.

Blacksmiths with grimed and hairy chests environ
   the anvil,
Each has his main-sledge . . . . they are all out
   . . . . there is a great heat in the fire.

From the cinder-strewed threshold I follow their
   movements,
The lithe sheer of their waists plays even with their
   massive arms,
Overhand the hammers roll—overhand so slow—
   overhand so sure,
They do not hasten, each man hits in his place.

[13] The negro holds firmly the reins of his four horses
   . . . . the block swags underneath on its tied-over
   chain,
The negro that drives the huge dray of the stoneyard
   . . . . steady and tall he stands poised on one leg
   on the stringpiece,   220
His blue shirt exposes his ample neck and breast and
   loosens over his hipband,

212 **shuffle and breakdown** popular dances often featured in contemporary minstrels 219 **swags** sways 220 **dray** cart used to haul heavy loads **stringpiece** long piece of heavy timber used in construction

28   *Walt Whitman*

His glance is calm and commanding . . . . he tosses
    the slouch of his hat away from his forehead,
The sun falls on his crispy hair and moustache . . . .
    falls on the black of his polish'd and perfect limbs.

I behold the picturesque giant and love him . . . .
    and I do not stop there,
I go with the team also.

In me the caresser of life wherever moving . . . .
    backward as well as forward slueing,
To niches aside and junior bending.

Oxen that rattle the yoke or halt in the shade, what
    is that you express in your eyes?
It seems to me more than all the print I have read
    in my life.

My tread scares the wood-drake and wood-duck on
    my distant and daylong ramble,   230
They rise together, they slowly circle around.

. . . . I believe in those winged purposes,
And acknowledge the red yellow and white playing
    within me,
And consider the green and violet and the tufted
    crown intentional;
And do not call the tortoise unworthy because she is
    not something else,
And the mocking bird in the swamp never studied
    the gamut, yet trills pretty well to me,
And the look of the bay mare shames silliness out of
    me.

[14] The wild gander leads his flock through the cool
    night,
Ya-honk! he says, and sounds it down to me like an
    invitation;

236 **gamut** the entire musical scale

Song of Myself 29

The pert may suppose it meaningless, but I listen
closer,
I find its purpose and place up there toward the
November sky.

The sharphoofed moose of the north, the cat on the
housesill, the chickadee, the prairie-dog,
The litter of the grunting sow as they tug at her teats,
The brood of the turkeyhen, and she with her
halfspread wings,
I see in them and myself the same old law.

The press of my foot to the earth springs a hundred
affections,
They scorn the best I can do to relate them.

I am enamoured of growing outdoors,
Of men that live among cattle or taste of the ocean
or woods,
Of the builders and steerers of ships, of the wielders
of axes and mauls, of the drivers of horses,
I can eat and sleep with them week in and week out.

What is commonest and cheapest and nearest and
easiest is Me,
Me going in for my chances, spending for vast
returns,
Adorning myself to bestow myself on the first that
will take me,
Not asking the sky to come down to my goodwill,
Scattering it freely forever.

[15]   The pure contralto sings in the organloft,
The carpenter dresses his plank . . . . the tongue
of his foreplane whistles its wild ascending lisp,
The married and unmarried children ride home to
their thanksgiving dinner,
The pilot seizes the king-pin, he heaves down with a
strong arm,
The mate stands braced in the whaleboat, lance and
harpoon are ready,

The duck-shooter walks by silent and cautious stretches,
The deacons are ordained with crossed hands at the altar,
The spinning-girl retreats and advances to the hum of the big wheel,
The farmer stops by the bars of a Sunday and looks at the oats and rye,
The lunatic is carried at last to the asylum a confirmed case,
He will never sleep any more as he did in the cot in his mother's bedroom;
The jour printer with gray head and gaunt jaws works at his case,
He turns his quid of tobacco, his eyes get blurred with the manuscript;
The malformed limbs are tied to the anatomist's table, 270
What is removed drops horribly in a pail;
The quadroon girl is sold at the stand .... the drunkard nods by the barroom stove,
The machinist rolls up his sleeves .... the policeman travels his beat .... the gatekeeper marks who pass,
The young fellow drives the express-wagon .... I love him though I do not know him;
The half-breed straps on his light boots to compete in the race,
The western turkey-shooting draws old and young .... some lean on their rifles, some sit on logs,
Out from the crowd steps the marksman and takes his position and levels his piece;
The groups of newly-come immigrants cover the wharf or levee,
The woollypates hoe in the sugarfield, the overseer views them from his saddle;
The bugle calls in the ballroom, the gentlemen run for their partners, the dancers bow to each other; 280

268 **jour printer** journeyman printer   272 **quadroon** offspring of a mulatto and a white person   279 **woollypates** Negroes

Song of Myself 31

The youth lies awake in the cedar-roofed garret and
  harks to the musical rains,
The Wolverine sets traps on the creek that helps fill
  the Huron,
The reformer ascends the platform, he spouts with his
  mouth and nose,
The company returns from its excursion, the darkey
  brings up the rear and bears the well-riddled target,
The squaw wrapt in her yellow-hemmed cloth is
  offering moccasins and beadbags for sale,
The connoisseur peers along the exhibition-gallery
  with halfshut eyes bent sideways,
The deckhands make fast the steamboat, the plank is
  thrown for the shoregoing passengers,
The young sister holds out the skein, the elder sister
  winds it off in a ball and stops now and then for
  the knots,
The one-year wife is recovering and happy, a week ago
  she bore her first child,
The cleanhaired Yankee girl works with her
  sewing-machine or in the factory or mill,   290
The nine months' gone is in the parturition chamber,
  her faintness and pains are advancing;
The pavingman leans on his twohanded rammer—
  the reporter's lead flies swiftly over the notebook
  —the signpainter is lettering with red and gold,
The canal-boy trots on the towpath—the bookkeeper
  counts at his desk—the shoemaker waxes his thread,
The conductor beats time for the band and all the
  performers follow him,
The child is baptised—the convert is making the first
  professions,
The regatta is spread on the bay . . . . how the
  white sails sparkle!
The drover watches his drove, he sings out to them
  that would stray,
The pedlar sweats with his pack on his back—the
  purchaser higgles about the odd cent,
The camera and plate are prepared, the lady must sit
  for her daguerreotype,

282 **Wolverine** native of Michigan 298 **higgles** bargains for small advantage

The bride unrumples her white dress, the minutehand
of the clock moves slowly,
The opium eater reclines with rigid head and
just-opened lips,
The prostitute draggles her shawl, her bonnet bobs
on her tipsy and pimpled neck,
The crowd laugh at her blackguard oaths, the men
jeer and wink to each other,
(Miserable! I do not laugh at your oaths nor jeer you,)
The President holds a cabinet council, he is
surrounded by the great secretaries,
On the piazza walk five friendly matrons with twined
arms;
The crew of the fish-smack pack repeated layers of
halibut in the hold,
The Missourian crosses the plains toting his wares and
his cattle,
The fare-collector goes through the train—he gives
notice by the jingling of loose change,
The floormen are laying the floor—the tinners are
tinning the roof—the masons are calling for mortar,
In single file each shouldering his hod pass onward
the laborers;
Seasons pursuing each other the indescribable crowd
is gathered . . . . it is the Fourth of July . . . .
what salutes of cannon and small arms!
Seasons pursuing each other the plougher ploughs
and the mower mows and the wintergrain falls in
the ground;
Off on the lakes the pikefisher watches and waits by
the hole in the frozen surface,
The stumps stand thick round the clearing, the
squatter strikes deep with his axe,
The flatboatmen make fast toward dusk near the
cottonwood or pekantrees,
The coon-seekers go now through the regions of the
Red river, or through those drained by the Tennessee,
or through those of the Arkansas,
The torches shine in the dark that hangs on the
Chattahoochee or Altamahaw;

318 **Chattahoochee or Altamahaw** rivers in Georgia

Patriarchs sit at supper with sons and grandsons and
    great grandsons around them,
In walls of adobie, in canvas tents, rest hunters and
    trappers after their day's sport.
The city sleeps and the country sleeps,
The living sleep for their time . . . . the dead sleep
    for their time,
The old husband sleeps by his wife and the young
    husband sleeps by his wife;
And these one and all tend inward to me, and I tend
    outward to them,
And such as it is to be of these more or less I am.

[16] I am of old and young, of the foolish as much as the
    wise,
Regardless of others, ever regardful of others,
Maternal as well as paternal, a child as well as a man,
Stuffed with the stuff that is coarse, and stuffed with
    the stuff that is fine,
One of the great nations, the nation of many nations
    —the smallest the same and the largest the same,
A southerner soon as a northerner, a planter nonchalant
    and hospitable,
A Yankee bound my own way . . . . ready for trade
    . . . . my joints the limberest joints on earth and
    the sternest joints on earth,
A Kentuckian walking the vale of the Elkhorn in my
    deerskin leggings,
A boatman over the lakes or bays or along coasts
    . . . . a Hoosier, a Badger, a Buckeye,
A Louisianian or Georgian, a poke-easy from sandhills
    and pines,
At home on Canadian snowshoes or up in the bush,
    or with fishermen off Newfoundland,
At home in the fleet of iceboats, sailing with the rest
    and tacking,
At home on the hills of Vermont or in the woods of
    Maine or the Texan ranch,

334 **a Hoosier, a Badger, a Buckeye** natives of Indiana, Wisconsin, and Ohio, respectively   335 **poke-easy** easy-going or lazy person

Comrade of Californians . . . . comrade of free
   northwesterners, loving their big proportions,
Comrade of raftsmen and coalmen—comrade of all
   who shake hands and welcome to drink and meat;   340
A learner with the simplest, a teacher of the
   thoughtfulest,
A novice beginning experient of myriads of seasons,
Of every hue and trade and rank, of every caste and
   religion,
Not merely of the New World but of Africa Europe
   or Asia . . . . a wandering savage,
A farmer, mechanic, or artist . . . . a gentleman,
   sailor, lover or quaker,
A prisoner, fancy-man, rowdy, lawyer, physician or
   priest.

I resist anything better than my own diversity,
And breathe the air and leave plenty after me,
And am not stuck up, and am in my place.

The moth and the fisheggs are in their place,   350
The suns I see and the suns I cannot see are in their
   place,
The palpable is in its place and the impalpable is in its
   place.

[17] These are the thoughts of all men in all ages and
   lands, they are not original with me,
If they are not yours as much as mine they are
   nothing or next to nothing,
If they do not enclose everything they are next to
   nothing,
If they are not the riddle and the untying of the
   riddle they are nothing,
If they are not just as close as they are distant they are
   nothing.

346 **fancy-man** a pimp or male sweetheart

Song of Myself   35

This is the grass that grows wherever the land is and the water is,
This is the common air that bathes the globe.

This is the breath of laws and songs and behaviour,   360
This is the tasteless water of souls . . . . this is the true sustenance,
It is for the illiterate . . . . it is for the judges of the supreme court . . . . it is for the federal capitol and the state capitols,
It is for the admirable communes of literary men and composers and singers and lecturers and engineers and savans,
It is for the endless races of working people and farmers and seamen.

[18] This is the trill of a thousand clear cornets and scream of the octave flute and strike of triangles.
I play not a march for victors only . . . . I play great marches for conquered and slain persons.

Have you heard that it was good to gain the day?
I also say it is good to fall . . . . battles are lost in the same spirit in which they are won.

I sound triumphal drums for the dead . . . . I fling through my embouchures the loudest and gayest music to them,
Vivas to those who have failed, and to those whose war-vessels sank in the sea, and those themselves who sank in the sea,
And to all generals that lost engagements, and all   370
overcome heroes, and the numberless unknown heroes equal to the greatest heroes known.

[19] This is the meal pleasantly set . . . . this is the meat and drink for natural hunger,

369 **embouchures** mouthpieces of wind instruments, or the shape of the mouth

36   Walt Whitman

It is for the wicked just the same as the righteous . . . .
    I make appointments with all,
I will not have a single person slighted or left away,
The keptwoman and sponger and thief are hereby invited
    . . . . the heavy-lipped slave is invited . . . . the
    venerealee is invited,
There shall be no difference between them and the rest.

This is the press of a bashful hand . . . . this is the float
    and odor of hair,
This is the touch of my lips to yours . . . . this is the
    murmur of yearning,
This is the far-off depth and height reflecting my own face,
This is the thoughtful merge of myself and the outlet
    again.   380

Do you guess I have some intricate purpose?
Well I have . . . . for the April rain has, and the mica
    on the side of a rock has.

Do you take it I would astonish?
Does the daylight astonish? or the early redstart
    twittering through the woods?
Do I astonish more than they?

This hour I tell things in confidence,
I might not tell everybody but I will tell you.

[20]   Who goes there! hankering, gross, mystical, nude?
How is it I extract strength from the beef I eat?

What is a man anyhow? What am I? and what are you?   390
All I mark as my own you shall offset it with your own,
Else it were time lost listening to me.

I do not snivel that snivel the world over,

388–389 This passage has been set to music by the American
composer Charles Ives (1874–1954).

That months are vacuums and the ground but wallow and
    filth,
That life is a suck and a sell, and nothing remains at the
    end but threadbare crape and tears.

Whimpering and truckling fold with powders for invalids
    . . . . conformity goes to the fourth-removed,
I cock my hat as I please indoors or out.

Shall I pray? Shall I venerate and be ceremonious?
I have pried through the strata and analyzed to a hair,
And counselled with doctors and calculated close and
    found no sweeter fat than sticks to my own bones.   400

In all people I see myself, none more and not one a
    barleycorn less,
And the good or bad I say of myself I say of them.

And I know I am solid and sound,
To me the converging objects of the universe perpetually
    flow,
All are written to me, and I must get what the writing
    means.

And I know I am deathless,
I know this orbit of mine cannot be swept by a carpenter's
    compass,
I know I shall not pass like a child's carlacue cut with a
    burnt stick at night.

I know I am august,
I do not trouble my spirit to vindicate itself or be
    understood,   410
I see that the elementary laws never apologize,
I reckon I behave no prouder than the level I plant my
    house by after all.

396 **truckling . . . powders** powdered medicine was often
folded in small papers 408 **carlacue** variant of curlicue

38 Walt Whitman

I exist as I am, that is enough,
If no other in the world be aware I sit content,
And if each and all be aware I sit content.

One world is aware, and by far the largest to me, and that
   is myself,
And whether I come to my own today or in ten thousand
   or ten million years,
I can cheerfully take it now, or with equal cheerfulness
   I can wait.

My foothold is tenoned and mortised in granite,
I laugh at what you call dissolution,   420
And I know the amplitude of time.

[21] I am the poet of the body,
And I am the poet of the soul.

The pleasures of heaven are with me, and the pains of hell
   are with me,
The first I graft and increase upon myself . . . . the
   latter I translate into a new tongue.

I am the poet of the woman the same as the man,
And I say it is as great to be a woman as to be a man,
And I say there is nothing greater than the mother of
   men.

I chant a new chant of dilation or pride,
We have had ducking and deprecating about enough,   430
I show that size is only development.

Have you outstript the rest? Are you the President?
It is a trifle . . . . they will more than arrive there every
   one, and still pass on.

I am he that walks with the tender and growing night;
I call to the earth and sea half-held by the night.

Press close barebosomed night! Press close magnetic
   nourishing night!

Song of Myself   39

Night of south winds! Night of the large few stars!
Still nodding night! Mad naked summer night!

Smile O voluptuous coolbreathed earth!
Earth of the slumbering and liquid trees!   440
Earth of departed sunset! Earth of the mountains
    misty-topt!
Earth of the vitreous pour of the full moon just tinged
    with blue!
Earth of shine and dark mottling the tide of the river!
Earth of the limpid gray of clouds brighter and clearer
    for my sake!
Far-swooping elbowed earth! Rich apple-blossomed earth!
Smile, for your lover comes!

Prodigal! you have given me love! . . . . therefore I to
    you give love!
O unspeakable passionate love!

Thruster holding me tight and that I hold tight!
We hurt each other as the bridegroom and the bride hurt
    each other.   450

[22] You sea! I resign myself to you also . . . . I guess what
    you mean,
I behold from the beach your crooked inviting fingers,
I believe you refuse to go back without feeling of me;
We must have a turn together . . . . I undress . . . .
    hurry me out of sight of the land,
Cushion me soft . . . . rock me in billowy drowse,
Dash me with amorous wet . . . . I can repay you.

Sea of stretched ground-swells!
Sea breathing broad and convulsive breaths!
Sea of the brine of life! Sea of unshovelled and
    always-ready graves!
Howler and scooper of storms! Capricious and dainty sea! 460
I am integral with you . . . . I too am of one phase and
    of all phases.

Partaker of influx and efflux . . . . extoller of hate and
  conciliation,
Extoller of amies and those that sleep in each others' arms.

I am he attesting sympathy;
Shall I make my list of things in the house and skip the
  house that supports them?

I am the poet of commonsense and of the demonstrable
  and of immortality;
And am not the poet of goodness only . . . . I do not
  decline to be the poet of wickedness also.

Washes and razors for foofoos . . . . for me freckles
  and a bristling beard.

What blurt is it about virtue and about vice?
Evil propels me, and reform of evil propels me . . . .
  I stand indifferent,   470
My gait is no faultfinder's or rejecter's gait,
I moisten the roots of all that has grown.

Did you fear some scrofula out of the unflagging
  pregnancy?
Did you guess the celestial laws are yet to be worked over
  and rectified?

I step up to say that what we do is right and what we
  affirm is right . . . . and some is only the ore of right,
Witnesses of us . . . . one side a balance and the
  antipodal side a balance,
Soft doctrine as steady help as stable doctrine,
Thoughts and deeds of the present our rouse and early
  start.

This minute that comes to me over the past decillions,
There is no better than it and now.   480

463 **amies** friends or lovers (French) 468 **foofoos** slang for
fools or perhaps fops

Song of Myself   41

What behaved well in the past or behaves well today is
  not such a wonder,
The wonder is always and always how there can be a mean
  man or an infidel.

[23] Endless unfolding of words of ages!
And mine a word of the modern . . . . a word en masse.

A word of the faith that never balks,
One time as good as another time . . . . here or
  henceforward it is all the same to me.

A word of reality . . . . materialism first and last
  imbuing.

Hurrah for positive science! Long live exact demonstration!
Fetch stonecrop and mix it with cedar and branches of
  lilac;
This is the lexicographer or chemist . . . . this made a
  grammar of the old cartouches,   490
These mariners put the ship through dangerous unknown
  seas,
This is the geologist, and this works with the scalpel, and
  this is a mathematician.

Gentlemen I receive you, and attach and clasp hands
  with you,
The facts are useful and real . . . . they are not my
  dwelling . . . . I enter by them to an area of the
  dwelling.

I am less the reminder of property or qualities, and more
  the reminder of life,

484 **en masse** all together, in the mass (French)   489 **stonecrop**
mossy creeping sedum with pungent fleshy leaves and yellow flowers   490 **cartouches** oval or oblong figures on ancient Egyptian
monuments enclosing a ruler's name

And go on the square for my own sake and for other's sake,
And make short account of neuters and geldings, and
    favor men and women fully equipped,
And beat the gong of revolt, and stop with fugitives and
    them that plot and conspire.

[24] Walt Whitman, an American, one of the roughs,
    a kosmos,
   Disorderly fleshy and sensual . . . . eating drinking
       and breeding,
   No sentimentalist . . . . no stander above men and
       women or apart from them . . . . no more modest
       than immodest.

Unscrew the locks from the doors!
Unscrew the doors themselves from their jambs!

Whoever degrades another degrades me . . . . and
    whatever is done or said returns at last to me,
And whatever I do or say I also return.

Through me the afflatus surging and surging . . . .
    through me the current and index.

I speak the password primeval . . . . I give the sign of
    democracy;
By God! I will accept nothing which all cannot have their
    counterpart of on the same terms.

Through me many long dumb voices,
Voices of the interminable generations of slaves,
Voices of prostitutes and of deformed persons,
Voices of the diseased and despairing, and of thieves and
    dwarfs,
Voices of cycles of preparation and accretion,
And of the threads that connect the stars—and of wombs,
    and of the fatherstuff,
And of the rights of them the others are down upon,

499 **kosmos** cosmos, a self-contained entity

Of the trivial and flat and foolish and despised,
Of fog in the air and beetles rolling balls of dung.

Through me forbidden voices,
Voices of sexes and lusts . . . . voices veiled, and I
 remove the veil,
Voices indecent by me clarified and transfigured.

I do not press my finger across my mouth,
I keep as delicate around the bowels as around the head
 and heart,
Copulation is no more rank to me than death is.

I believe in the flesh and the appetites,
Seeing hearing and feeling are miracles, and each part and
 tag of me is a miracle.

Divine am I inside and out, and I make holy whatever
 I touch or am touched from;
The scent of these arm-pits is aroma finer than prayer,
This head is more than churches or bibles or creeds.

If I worship any particular thing it shall be some of the
 spread of my body;
Translucent mould of me it shall be you,
Shaded ledges and rests, firm masculine coulter, it shall
 be you,
Whatever goes to the tilth of me it shall be you,
You my rich blood, your milky stream pale strippings of
 my life;
Breast that presses against other breasts it shall be you,
My brain it shall be your occult convolutions,
Root of washed sweet-flag, timorous pond-snipe, nest of
 guarded duplicate eggs, it shall be you,
Mixed tussled hay of head and beard and brawn it shall
 be you,

530 **Translucent mould** semen   531 **coulter** knife attached to
the front of a plow, the phallus   532 **tilth** cultivated or tilled
soil, literally   536 **sweet-flag . . . eggs** phallic images

Trickling sap of maple, fibre of manly wheat, it shall
   be you;
Sun so generous it shall be you,
Vapors lighting and shading my face it shall be you,   540
You sweaty brooks and dews it shall be you,
Winds whose soft-tickling genitals rub against me it shall
   be you,
Broad muscular fields, branches of liveoak, loving lounger
   in my winding paths, it shall be you,
Hands I have taken, face I have kissed, mortal I have
   ever touched, it shall be you.

I dote on myself . . . . there is that lot of me, and all
   so luscious,
Each moment and whatever happens thrills me with joy.

I cannot tell how my ankles bend . . . . nor whence
   the cause of my faintest wish,
Nor the cause of the friendship I emit . . . . nor the
   cause of the friendship I take again.

To walk up my stoop is unaccountable . . . . I pause
   to consider if it really be,
That I eat and drink is spectacle enough for the great
   authors and schools,   550
A morning-glory at my window satisfies me more than the
   metaphysics of books.

To behold the daybreak!
The little light fades the immense and diaphanous
   shadows,
The air tastes good to my palate.

Hefts of the moving world at innocent gambols, silently
   rising, freshly exuding,
Scooting obliquely high and low.

Something I cannot see puts upward libidinous prongs,
Seas of bright juice suffuse heaven.

555 **Hefts** mass, main part

Song of Myself 45

The earth by the sky staid with .... the daily close
  of their junction,
The heaved challenge from the east that moment over
  my head,
The mocking taunt, See then whether you shall be master!

[25] Dazzling and tremendous how quick the sunrise would
  kill me,
If I could not now and always send sunrise out of me.

We also ascend dazzling and tremendous as the sun,
We found our own my soul in the calm and cool of the
  daybreak.

My voice goes after what my eyes cannot reach,
With the twirl of my tongue I encompass worlds and
  volumes of worlds.

Speech is the twin of my vision .... it is unequal to
  measure itself.
It provokes me forever,
It says sarcastically, Walt, you understand enough ....
  why don't you let it out then?

Come now I will not be tantalized .... you conceive
  too much of articulation.

Do you not know how the buds beneath are folded?
Waiting in gloom protected by frost,
The dirt receding before my prophetical screams,
I underlying causes to balance them at last,
My knowledge my live parts .... it keeping tally with
  the meaning of things,
Happiness .... which whoever hears me let him or
  her set out in search of this day.

My final merit I refuse you .... I refuse putting from
  me the best I am.

Encompass worlds but never try to encompass me,
I crowd your noisiest talk by looking toward you.

46   Walt Whitman

Writing and talk do not prove me,
I carry the plenum of proof and every thing else in my
   face,
With the hush of my lips I confound the topmost skeptic.

[26] I think I will do nothing for a long time but listen,
And accrue what I hear into myself . . . . and let
   sounds contribute toward me.

I hear the bravuras of birds . . . . the bustle of growing
   wheat . . . . gossip of flames . . . . clack of sticks
   cooking my meals.

I hear the sound of the human voice . . . . a sound
   I love,
I hear all sounds as they are tuned to their uses . . . .
   sounds of the city and sounds out of the city . . . .
   sounds of the day and night;
Talkative young ones to those that like them . . . .
   the recitative of fish-pedlars and fruit-pedlars . . . .
   the loud laugh of workpeople at their meals,
The angry base of disjointed friendship . . . . the faint
   tones of the sick,
The judge with hands tight to the desk, his shaky lips
   pronouncing a death-sentence,
The heave'e'yo of stevedores unlading ships by the
   wharves . . . . the refrain of the anchor-lifters;
The ring of alarm-bells . . . . the cry of fire . . . .
   the whirr of swift-streaking engines and hose-carts
   with premonitory tinkles and colored lights,
The steam-whistle . . . . the solid roll of the train of
   approaching cars;
The slow-march played at night at the head of the
   association,
They go to guard some corpse . . . . the flag-tops are
   draped with black muslin.

I hear the violincello or man's heart complaint,
And hear the keyed cornet or else the echo of sunset.

582 **plenum** fullness

I hear the chorus . . . . it is a grand-opera . . . . this
   indeed is music!

A tenor large and fresh as the creation fills me,   600
The orbic flex of his mouth is pouring and filling me full.

I hear the trained soprano . . . . she convulses me like
   the climax of my love-grip;
The orchestra whirls me wider than Uranus flies,
It wrenches unnamable ardors from my breast,
It throbs me to gulps of the farthest down horror,
It sails me . . . . I dab with bare feet . . . . they are
   licked by the indolent waves,
I am exposed . . . . cut by bitter and poisoned hail,
Steeped amid honeyed morphine . . . . my windpipe
   squeezed in the fakes of death,
Let up again to feel the puzzle of puzzles,
And that we call Being.   610

[27] To be in any form, what is that?
If nothing lay more developed the quahaug and its callous
   shell were enough.

Mine is no callous shell,
I have instant conductors all over me whether I pass or
   stop,
They seize every object and lead it harmlessly through me.

I merely stir, press, feel with my fingers, and am happy,
To touch my person to some one else's is about as much
   as I can stand.

[28] Is this then a touch? . . . . quivering me to a new
   identity,
Flames and ether making a rush for my veins,
Treacherous tip of me reaching and crowding to help
   them,   620

612 **quahaug** thick-shelled American clam

48   Walt Whitman

My flesh and blood playing out lightning, to strike what
    is hardly different from myself,
On all sides prurient provokers stiffening my limbs,
Straining the udder of my heart for its withheld drip,
Behaving licentious toward me, taking no denial,
Depriving me of my best as for a purpose,
Unbuttoning my clothes and holding me by the bare
    waist,
Deluding my confusion with the calm of the sunlight
    and pasture fields,
Immodestly sliding the fellow-senses away,
They bribed to swap off with touch, and go and graze at
    the edges of me,
No consideration, no regard for my draining strength or
    my anger,   630
Fetching the rest of the herd around to enjoy them awhile,
Then all uniting to stand on a headland and worry me.

The sentries desert every other part of me,
They have left me helpless to a red marauder,
They all come to the headland to witness and assist
    against me.
I am given up by traitors;
I talk wildly . . . . I have lost my wits . . . . I and
    nobody else am the greatest traitor,
I went myself first to the headland . . . . my own hands
    carried me there.

You villain touch! what are you doing? . . . . my breath
    is tight in its throat;
Unclench your floodgates! you are too much for me.   640

[29] Blind loving wrestling touch! Sheathed hooded
        sharptoothed touch!
Did it make you ache so leaving me?

Parting tracked by arriving . . . . perpetual payment
    of the perpetual loan,

   634 **marauder**   plunderer, like the Indian

Rich showering rain, and recompense richer afterward.

Sprouts take and accumulate . . . . stand by the curb
    prolific and vital,
Landscapes projected masculine full-sized and golden.

[30] All truths wait in all things,
They neither hasten their own delivery nor resist it,
They do not need the obstetric forceps of the surgeon,
The insignificant is as big to me as any,
What is less or more than a touch?

Logic and sermons never convince,
The damp of the night drives deeper into my soul.

Only what proves itself to every man and woman is so,
Only what nobody denies is so.

A minute and a drop of me settle my brain;
I believe the soggy clods shall become lovers and lamps,
And a compend of compends is the meat of a man or
    woman,
And a summit and flower there is the feeling they have for
    each other,
And they are to branch boundlessly out of that lesson
    until it becomes omnific,
And until every one shall delight us, and we them.

[31] I believe a leaf of grass is no less than the journeywork
    of the stars,
And the pismire is equally perfect, and a grain of sand,
    and the egg of the wren,
And the tree-toad is a chef-d'œuvre for the highest,
And the running blackberry would adorn the parlors
    of heaven,

---

645 **curb** womb   658 **compend** compendium   660 **omnific**
unlimited in creative power   663 **pismire** ant   664 **chef-
d'œuvre** masterpiece (French)

50 Walt Whitman

And the narrowest hinge in my hand puts to scorn all
    machinery,
And the cow crunching with depressed head surpasses any
    statue,
And a mouse is miracle enough to stagger sextillions
    of infidels,
And I could come every afternoon of my life to look at
    the farmer's girl boiling her iron tea-kettle and baking
    shortcake.

I find I incorporate gneiss and coal and long-threaded
    moss and fruits and grains and esculent roots,   670
And am stucco'd with quadrupeds and birds all over,
And have distanced what is behind me for good reasons,
And call any thing close again when I desire it.

In vain the speeding or shyness,
In vain the plutonic rocks send their old heat against
    my approach,
In vain the mastodon retreats beneath its own powdered
    bones,
In vain objects stand leagues off and assume manifold
    shapes,
In vain the ocean settling in hollows and the great
    monsters lying low,
In vain the buzzard houses herself with the sky,
In vain the snake slides through the creepers and logs,   680
In vain the elk takes to the inner passes of the woods,
In vain the razorbilled auk sails far north to Labrador,
I follow quickly . . . . I ascend to the nest in the fissure
    of the cliff.

[32] I think I could turn and live awhile with the animals
       . . . . they are so placid and self-contained,
I stand and look at them sometimes half the day long.

They do not sweat and whine about their condition,
They do not lie awake in the dark and weep for their sins,
They do not make me sick discussing their duty to God,
Not one is dissatisfied . . . . not one is demented with
    the mania of owning things,

Song of Myself 51

Not one kneels to another nor to his kind that lived
 thousands of years ago, 690
Not one is respectable or industrious over the whole earth.

So they show their relations to me and I accept them;
They bring me tokens of myself . . . . they evince them
 plainly in their possession.

I do not know where they got those tokens,
I must have passed that way untold times ago and
 negligently dropt them,
Myself moving forward then and now and forever,
Gathering and showing more always and with velocity,
Infinite and omnigenous and the like of these among
 them;
Not too exclusive toward the reachers of my
 remembrancers,
Picking out here one that shall be my amie, 700
Choosing to go with him on brotherly terms.

A gigantic beauty of a stallion, fresh and responsive to my
 caresses,
Head high in the forehead and wide between the ears,
Limbs glossy and supple, tail dusting the ground,
Eyes well apart and full of sparkling wickedness . . . .
 ears finely cut and flexibly moving.

His nostrils dilate . . . . my heels embrace him . . . .
 his well built limbs tremble with pleasure . . . . we
 speed around and return.

I but use you a moment and then I resign you stallion
 . . . . and do not need your paces, and outgallop
 them,
And myself as I stand or sit pass faster than you.

[33] Swift wind! Space! My Soul! Now I know it is true what
 I guessed at;
What I guessed when I loafed on the grass, 710

698 **omnigenous** composed of all varieties 700 **amie** brother
or friend (feminine form is obviously an error)

52   Walt Whitman

What I guessed while I lay alone in my bed . . . . and
  again as I walked the beach under the paling stars
  of the morning.

My ties and ballasts leave me . . . . I travel . . . .
  I sail . . . . my elbows rest in the sea-gaps,
I skirt the sierras . . . . my palms cover continents,
I am afoot with my vision.

By the city's quadrangular houses . . . . in log-huts, or
  camping with lumbermen,
Along the ruts of the turnpike . . . . along the dry gulch
  and rivulet bed,
Hoeing my onion-patch, and rows of carrots and parsnips
  . . . . crossing savannas . . . . trailing in forests,
Prospecting . . . . gold-digging . . . . girdling the trees
  of a new purchase,
Scorched ankle-deep by the hot sand . . . . hauling my
  boat down the shallow river;
Where the panther walks to and fro on a limb overhead
  . . . . where the buck turns furiously at the hunter,   720
Where the rattlesnake suns his flabby length on a rock
  . . . . where the otter is feeding on fish,
Where the alligator in his tough pimples sleeps by the
  bayou,
Where the black bear is searching for roots or honey
  . . . . where the beaver pats the mud with his
  paddle-tail;
Over the growing sugar . . . . over the cottonplant
  . . . . over the rice in its low moist field;
Over the sharp-peaked farmhouse with its scalloped scum
  and slender shoots from the gutters;
Over the western persimmon . . . . over the longleaved
  corn and the delicate blue-flowered flax;
Over the white and brown buckwheat, a hummer and a
  buzzer there with the rest,
Over the dusky green of the rye as it ripples and shades
  in the breeze;

712 **ties and ballasts** the release of a balloon   725 **scalloped
scum** foam on the roof of farmhouse with wooden roof

Scaling mountains . . . . pulling myself cautiously up
    . . . . holding on by low scragged limbs,
Walking the path worn in the grass and beat through the
    leaves of the brush;
Where the quail is whistling betwixt the woods and the
    wheatlot,
Where the bat flies in the July eve . . . . where the great
    goldbug drops through the dark;
Where the flails keep time on the barn floor,
Where the brook puts out of the roots of the old tree and
    flows to the meadow,
Where cattle stand and shake away flies with the
    tremulous shuddering of their hides,
Where the cheese-cloth hangs in the kitchen, and
    andirons straddle the hearth-slab, and cobwebs fall
    in festoons from the rafters;
Where triphammers crash . . . . where the press is
    whirling its cylinders;
Wherever the human heart beats with terrible throes out
    of its ribs;
Where the pear-shaped balloon is floating aloft . . . .
    floating in it myself and looking composedly down;
Where the life-car is drawn on the slipnoose . . . .
    where the heat hatches pale-green eggs in the dented
    sand,
Where the she-whale swims with her calves and never
    forsakes them,
Where the steamship trails hindways its long pennant
    of smoke,
Where the ground-shark's fin cuts like a black chip out of
    the water,
Where the half-burned brig is riding on unknown curernts,
Where shells grow to her slimy deck, and the dead are
    corrupting below;
Where the striped and starred flag is borne at the head
    of the regiments;
Approaching Manhattan, up by the long-stretching island,

---

729 **scragged** scrawny   740 **life-car** watertight boat traveling
on a rope in order to haul a person through surf too heavy for
an open boat

Under Niagara, the cataract falling like a veil over my
  countenance;
Upon a door-step .... upon the horse-block of hard
  wood outside,
Upon the race-course, or enjoying pic-nics or jigs or a
  good game of base-ball,
At he-festivals with blackguard jibes and ironical license
  and bull-dances and drinking and laughter,
At the cider-mill, tasting the sweet of the brown sqush
  .... sucking the juice through a straw,
At apple-peelings, wanting kisses for all the red fruit I find,
At musters and beach-parties and friendly bees and
  huskings and house-raisings;
Where the mockingbird sounds his delicious gurgles, and
  cackles and screams and weeps,
Where the hay-rick stands in the barnyard, and the
  dry-stalks are scattered, and the brood cow waits in the
  hovel,
Where the bull advances to do his masculine work, and
  the stud to the mare, and the cock is treading the hen,
Where the heifers browse, and the geese nip their food
  with short jerks;
Where the sundown shadows lengthen over the limitless
  and lonesome prairie,
Where the herds of buffalo make a crawling spread of the
  square miles far and near;
Where the hummingbird shimmers .... where the
  neck of the longlived swan is curving and winding;
Where the laughing-gull scoots by the slappy shore and
  laughs her near-human laugh;
Where beehives range on a gray bench in the garden
  half-hid by the high weeds;
Where the band-necked partridges roost in a ring on the
  ground with their heads out;
Where burial coaches enter the arched gates of a cemetery;
Where winter wolves bark amid wastes of snow and
  icicled trees;
Where the yellow-crowned heron comes to the edge of the
  marsh at night and feeds upon small crabs;

751 **bull-dances** stag dances, possibly Indian buffalo dances, or
Dionysian rites   754 **musters** gatherings of people

Where the splash of swimmers and divers cools the warm noon;
Where the katydid works her chromatic reed on the walnut-tree over the well;
Through patches of citrons and cucumbers with silver-wired leaves,
Through the salt-lick or orange glade .... or under conical firs;
Through the gymnasium .... through the curtained saloon .... through the office or public hall;
Pleased with the native and pleased with the foreign .... pleased with the new and old,
Pleased with women, the homely as well as the handsome,
Pleased with the quakeress as she puts off her bonnet and talks melodiously,
Pleased with the primitive tunes of the choir of the whitewashed church,
Pleased with the earnest words of the sweating Methodist preacher, or any preacher .... looking seriously at the camp-meeting;
Looking in at the shop-windows in Broadway the whole forenoon .... pressing the flesh of my nose to the thick plate-glass,
Wandering the same afternoon with my face turned up to the clouds;
My right and left arms round the sides of two friends and I in the middle;
Coming home with the bearded and dark-cheeked bush-boy .... riding behind him at the drape of the day;
Far from the settlements studying the print of animals' feet, or the moccasin print;
By the cot in the hospital reaching lemonade to a feverish patient,
By the coffined corpse when all is still, examining with a candle;
Voyaging to every port to dicker and adventure;
Hurrying with the modern crowd, as eager and fickle as any,
Hot toward one I hate, ready in my madness to knife him;

781 **drape of the day** sunset

Solitary at midnight in my back yard, my thoughts gone
    from me a long while,
Walking the old hills of Judea with the beautiful gentle
    god by my side;
Speeding through space . . . . speeding through heaven
    and the stars,
Speeding amid the seven satellites and the broad ring and
    the diameter of eighty thousand miles,
Speeding with tailed meteors . . . . throwing fire-balls
    like the rest,
Carrying the crescent child that carries its own full mother
    in its belly:
Storming enjoying planning loving cautioning,
Backing and filling, appearing and disappearing,
I tread day and night such roads.

I visit the orchards of God and look at the spheric product,
And look at quintillions ripened, and look at quintillions
    green.

I fly the flight of the fluid and swallowing soul,
My course runs below the soundings of plummets.

I help myself to material and immaterial,
No guard can shut me off, no law can prevent me.

I anchor my ship for a little while only,
My messengers continually cruise away or bring their
    returns to me.

I go hunting polar furs and the seal . . . . leaping
    chasms with a pike-pointed staff . . . . clinging to
    topples of brittle and blue.

I ascend to the foretruck . . . . I take my place late at
    night in the crow's nest . . . . we sail through the
    arctic sea . . . . it is plenty light enough,
Through the clear atmosphere I stretch around on the
    wonderful beauty,

793 **Carrying . . . belly** lunar phases   806 **foretruck** truck at
the head of the foremast of ship

Song of Myself

The enormous masses of ice pass me and I pass them
 . . . . the scenery is plain in all directions,
The white-topped mountains point up in the distance
 . . . . I fling out my fancies toward them;
We are about approaching some great battlefield in which
 we are soon to be engaged,
We pass the colossal outposts of the encampment . . . .
 we pass with still feet and caution;
Or we are entering by the suburbs some vast and ruined
 city . . . . the blocks and fallen architecture more
 than all the living cities of the globe.

I am a free companion . . . . I bivouac by invading
 watchfires.

I turn the bridegroom out of bed and stay with the bride
 myself,
And tighten her all night to my thighs and lips.

My voice is the wife's voice, the screech by the rail of
 the stairs,
They fetch my man's body up dripping and drowned.
I understand the large hearts of heroes,
The courage of present times and all times;
How the skipper saw the crowded and rudderless wreck
 of the steamship, and death chasing it up and down
 the storm,
How he knuckled tight and gave not back one inch,
 and was faithful of days and faithful of nights,
And chalked in large letters on a board, Be of good cheer,
 We will not desert you;
How he saved the drifting company at last,
How the lank loose-gowned women looked when boated
 from the side of their prepared graves,
How the silent old-faced infants, and the lifted sick, and
 the sharp-lipped unshaved men;
All this I swallow and it tastes good . . . . I like it well,
 and it becomes mine,
I am the man . . . . I suffered . . . . I was there.

The disdain and calmness of martyrs,
The mother condemned for a witch and burnt with dry
  wood, and her children gazing on;
The hounded slave that flags in the race and leans by the
  fence, blowing and covered with sweat,   830
The twinges that sting like needles his legs and neck,
The murderous buckshot and the bullets,
All these I feel or am.

I am the hounded slave . . . . I wince at the bite of the
  dogs,
Hell and despair are upon me . . . . crack and again
  crack the marksmen,
I clutch the rails of the fence . . . . my gore dribs
  thinned with the ooze of my skin,
I fall on the weeds and stones,
The riders spur their unwilling horses and haul close,
They taunt my dizzy ears . . . . they beat me violently
  over the head with their whip-stocks.

Agonies are one of my changes of garments;   840
I do not ask the wounded person how he feels . . . .
  I myself become the wounded person,
My hurt turns livid upon me as I lean on a cane and
  observe.

I am the mashed fireman with breastbone broken . . . .
  tumbling walls buried me in their debris,
Heat and smoke I inspired . . . . I heard the yelling
  shouts of my comrades,
I heard the distant click of their picks and shovels;
They have cleared the beams away . . . . they tenderly
  lift me forth.

I lie in the night air in my red shirt . . . . the pervading
  hush is for my sake,
Painless after all I lie, exhausted but not so unhappy,
White and beautiful are the faces around me . . . .
  the heads are bared of their fire-caps,

836 **dribs** drops   844 **inspired** inhaled

The kneeling crowd fades with the light of the torches.

Distant and dead resuscitate,
They show as the dial or move as the hands of me . . . .
    and I am the clock myself.

I am an old artillerist, and tell of some fort's
    bombardment . . . . and am there again.

Again the reveille of drummers . . . . again the attacking
    cannon and mortars and howitzers,
Again the attacked send their cannon responsive.

I take part . . . . I see and hear the whole,
The cries and curses and roar . . . . the plaudits for
    well aimed shots,
The ambulanza slowly passing and trailing its red drip,
Workmen searching after damages and to make
    indispensable repairs,
The fall of grenades through the rent roof . . . . the
    fan-shaped explosion,
The whizz of limbs heads stone wood and iron high
    in the air.
Again gurgles the mouth of my dying general . . . .
    he furiously waves with his hand,
He gasps through the clot . . . . Mind not me . . . .
    mind . . . . the entrenchments.

[34] I tell not the fall of Alamo . . . . not one escaped to tell
    the fall of Alamo,
The hundred and fifty are dumb yet at Alamo.

Hear now the tale of a jetblack sunrise,
Hear of the murder in cold blood of four hundred and
    twelve young men.

858 **ambulanza** army ambulance   864ff. **Fall of Alamo** massacre of Texan soldiers on March 27, 1836

Retreating they had formed in a hollow square with
   their baggage for breastworks,
Nine hundred lives out of the surrounding enemy's nine
   times their number was the price they took in advance,
Their colonel was wounded and their ammunition gone, 870
They treated for an honorable capitulation, received
   writing and seal, gave up their arms, and marched
   back prisoners of war.

They were the glory of the race of rangers,
Matchless with a horse, a rifle, a song, a supper or a
   courtship,
Large, turbulent, brave, handsome, generous, proud and
   affectionate,
Bearded, sunburnt, dressed in the free costume of hunters,
Not a single one over thirty years of age.

The second Sunday morning they were brought out in
   squads and massacred . . . . it was beautiful early
   summer,
The work commenced about five o'clock and was over by
   eight.

None obeyed the command to kneel,
Some made a mad and helpless rush . . . . some stood
   stark and straight, 880
A few fell at once, shot in the temple or heart . . . .
   the living and dead lay together,
The maimed and mangled dug in the dirt . . . . the
   new-comers saw them there;
Some half-killed attempted to crawl away,
These were dispatched with bayonets or battered with the
   blunts of muskets;
A youth not seventeen years old seized his assassin till
   two more came to release him,
The three were all torn, and covered with the boy's
   blood.

At eleven o'clock began the burning of the bodies;
And that is the tale of the murder of the four hundred
   and twelve young men,
And that was a jetblack sunrise.

[35] Did you read in the seabooks of the oldfashioned frigate-fight?
Did you learn who won by the light of the moon and stars?

Our foe was no skulk in his ship, I tell you,
His was the English pluck, and there is no tougher or truer, and never was, and never will be;
Along the lowered eve he came, horribly raking us.

We closed with him . . . . the yards entangled . . . . the cannon touched,
My captain lashed fast with his own hands.

We had received some eighteen-pound shots under the water,
On our lower-gun-deck two large pieces had burst at the first fire, killing all around and blowing up overhead.

Ten o'clock at night, and the full moon shining and the leaks on the gain, and five feet of water reported,
The master-at-arms loosing the prisoners confined in the after-hold to give them a chance for themselves.

The transit to and from the magazine was now stopped by the sentinels,
They saw so many strange faces they did not know whom to trust.

Our frigate was afire . . . . the other asked if we demanded quarters? if our colors were struck and the fighting done?

I laughed content when I heard the voice of my little captain,
We have not struck, he composedly cried, We have just begun our part of the fighting.

890ff. John Paul Jones, in command of the *Bonhomme Richard*, defeated the British *Serapis* on September 23, 1779

Only three guns were in use,
One was directed by the captain himself against the
  enemy's mainmast,
Two well-served with grape and canister silenced his
  musketry and cleared his decks.

The tops alone seconded the fire of this little battery,
  especially the maintop,
They all held out bravely during the whole of the
  action.   910

Not a moment's cease,
The leaks gained fast on the pumps . . . . the fire eat
  toward the powder-magazine,
One of the pumps was shot away . . . . it was
  generally thought we were sinking.

Serene stood the little captain,
He was not hurried . . . . his voice was neither high
  nor low,
His eyes gave more light to us than our battle-lanterns.

Toward twelve at night, there in the beams of the moon
  they surrendered to us.

[36] Stretched and still lay the midnight,
Two great hulls motionless on the breast of the darkness,
Our vessel riddled and slowly sinking . . . . preparations
  to pass to the one we had conquered,   920
The captain on the quarter deck coldly giving his orders
  through a countenance white as a sheet,
Near by the corpse of the child that served in the cabin,
The dead face of an old salt with long white hair and
  carefully curled whiskers,
The flames spite of all that could be done flickering
  aloft and below,

908 **grape** grapeshot, a cluster of iron balls used as a charge
for a cannon   **canister** encased shot for close-range artillery fire

Song of Myself 63

The husky voices of the two or three officers yet fit
  for duty,
Formless stacks of bodies and bodies by themselves
  . . . . dabs of flesh upon the masts and spars,
The cut of cordage and dangle of rigging . . . . the
  slight shock of the soothe of waves,
Black and impressive guns, and litter of powder-parcels,
  and the strong scent,
Delicate sniffs of the seabreeze . . . . smells of sedgy
  grass and fields by the shore . . . . death-messages
  given in charge to survivors,
The hiss of the surgeon's knife and the gnawing teeth
  of his saw,
The wheeze, the cluck, the swash of falling blood
  . . . . the short wild scream, the long dull tapering
  groan,
These so . . . . these irretrievable.

[37] O Christ! My fit is mastering me!
What the rebel said gaily adjusting his throat to the
  rope-noose,
What the savage at the stump, his eye-sockets empty,
  his mouth spirting whoops and defiance,
What stills the traveler come to the vault at Mount
  Vernon,
What sobers the Brooklyn boy as he looks down the
  shores of the Wallabout and remembers the prison
  ships,
What burnt the gums of the redcoat at Saratoga when he
  surrendered his brigades,
These become mine and me every one, and they are
  but little,
I become as much more as I like.

I become any presence or truth of humanity here,
And see myself in prison shaped like another man,
And feel the dull unintermitted pain.
For me the keepers of convicts shoulder their carbines
  and keep watch,
It is I let out in the morning and barred at night.

Not a mutineer walks handcuffed to the jail, but I am
   handcuffed to him and walk by his side,
I am less the jolly one there, and more the silent one
   with sweat on my twitching lips.

Not a youngster is taken for larceny, but I go too and
   am tried and sentenced.

Not a cholera patient lies at the last gasp, but I also lie
   at the last gasp,
My face is ash-colored, my sinews gnarl . . . . away
   from me people retreat.   950

Askers embody themselves in me, and I am embodied
   in them,
I project my hat and sit shamefaced and beg.

I rise extatic through all, and sweep with the true
   gravitation,
The whirling and whirling is elemental within me.

[38] Somehow I have been stunned. Stand back!
Give me a little time beyond my cuffed head and
   slumbers and dreams and gaping,
I discover myself on a verge of the usual mistake.

That I could forget the mockers and insults!
That I could forget the trickling tears and the blows of
   the bludgeons and hammers!
That I could look with a separate look on my own
   crucifixion and bloody crowning!   960

I remember . . . . I resume the overstaid fraction,
The grave of rock multiplies what has been confided
   to it . . . . or to any graves,
The corpses rise . . . . the gashes heal . . . . the
   fastenings roll away.

I troop forth replenished with supreme power, one of
   an average unending procession,

We walk the roads of Ohio and Massachusetts and
    Virginia and Wisconsin and New York and New
    Orleans and Texas and Montreal and San Francisco
    and Charleston and Savannah and Mexico,
Inland and by the seacoast and boundary lines . . . .
    and we pass the boundary lines.

Our swift ordinances are on their way over the whole
    earth,
The blossoms we wear in our hats are the growth of
    two thousand years.

Eleves I salute you,
I see the approach of your numberless gangs I
    see you understand yourselves and me,   970
And know that they who have eyes are divine, and the
    blind and lame are equally divine,
And that my steps drag behind yours yet go before them,
And are aware how I am with you no more than I am
    with everybody.

[39] The friendly and flowing savage . . . . Who is he?
Is he waiting for civilization or past it and mastering it?

Is he some southwesterner raised outdoors? Is he
    Canadian?
Is he from the Mississippi country? or from Iowa,
    Oregon or California? or from the mountain? or
    prairie life or bush-life? or from the sea?

Wherever he goes men and women accept and desire
    him,
They desire he should like them and touch them and
    speak to them and stay with them.
Behaviour lawless as snow-flakes . . . . words simple
    as grass . . . . uncombed head and laughter and
    naivete;   980
Slowstepping feet and the common features, and the
    common modes and emanations,

969 **Eleves** pupils or disciples (French)

66   *Walt Whitman*

They descend in new forms from the tips of his
      fingers,
They are wafted with the odor of his body or breath
      . . . . they fly out of the glance of his eyes.

[40] Flaunt of the sunshine I need not your bask . . . .
      lie over,
You light surfaces only . . . . I force the surfaces and
      the depths also.

Earth! you seem to look for something at my hands,
Say old topknot! what do you want?

Man or woman! I might tell how I like you, but cannot,
And might tell what it is in me and what it is in you,
      but cannot,
And might tell the pinings I have . . . . the pulse of
      my nights and days.   990

Behold I do not give lectures or a little charity,
What I give I give out of myself.

You there, impotent, loose in the knees, open your
      scarfed chops till I blow grit within you,
Spread your palms and lift the flaps of your pockets,
I am not to be denied . . . . I compel . . . . I have
      stores plenty and to spare,
And any thing I have I bestow.

I do not ask who you are . . . . that is not important
      to me,
You can do nothing and be nothing but what I will
      infold you.

To a drudge of the cottonfields or emptier of privies I
      lean . . . . on his right cheek I put the family kiss,

987 **topknot** humorously compares earth to an Indian with a
tuft of hair on the top of his head   993 **scarfed chops** mouth
covered with a scarf or bandage, either a sick man or a corpse

And in my soul I swear I never will deny him.

On women fit for conception I start bigger and
    nimbler babes,
This day I am jetting the stuff of far more arrogant
    republics.

To any one dying . . . . thither I speed and twist the
    knob of the door,
Turn the bedclothes toward the foot of the bed,
Let the physician and the priest go home.

I seize the descending man . . . . I raise him with
    resistless will.

O despairer, here is my neck,
By God! you shall not go down! Hang your whole
    weight upon me.

I dilate you with tremendous breath . . . . I buoy
    you up;
Every room of the house do I fill with an armed force
    . . . . lovers of me, bafflers of graves:
Sleep! I and they keep guard all night;
Not doubt, not decease shall dare to lay finger upon you,
I have embraced you, and henceforth possess you to
    myself,
And when you rise in the morning you will find
    what I tell you is so.

[41] I am he bringing help for the sick as they pant on
    their backs,
And for strong upright men I bring yet more needed
    help.

I heard what was said of the universe,
Heard it and heard of several thousand years;
It is middling well as far as it goes . . . . but is that all?

Magnifying and applying come I, 1020
Outbidding at the start the old cautious hucksters,
The most they offer for mankind and eternity less
  than a spirt of my own seminal wet,
Taking myself the exact dimensions of Jehovah and
  laying them away,
Lithographing Kronos and Zeus his son, and Hercules
  his grandson,
Buying drafts of Osiris and Isis and Belus and Brahma
  and Adonai,
In my portfolio placing Manito loose, and Allah on a
  leaf, and the crucifix engraved,
With Odin, and the hideous-faced Mexitli, and all
  idols and images,
Honestly taking them all for what they are worth, and
  not a cent more,
Admitting they were alive and did the work of their day,
Admitting they bore mites as for unfledged birds who
  have now to rise and fly and sing for themselves, 1030
Accepting the rough deific sketches to fill out better in
  myself .... bestowing them freely on each man
  and woman I see,
Discovering as much or more in a framer framing a
  house,
Putting higher claims for him there with his rolled-up
  sleeves, driving the mallet and chisel;
Not objecting to special revelations .... considering a
  curl of smoke or a hair on the back of my hand as
  curious as any revelation;
Those ahold of fire-engines and hook-and-ladder ropes
  more to me than the gods of the antique wars,

1024 **Lithographing** making reproductions **Kronos** son of Uranus and Gaea (Greek) **Zeus** son of Kronos, who dethroned his father **Hercules** son of Zeus, the most famous Greek hero 1025 **Osiris** Egyptian god of the underworld **Isis** Egyptian goddess of fertility **Belus** son of Poseidon **Brahma** the first god of the Hindu trinity **Adonai** Hebrew name for God 1026 **Manito** Algonquian name for the spirit or force that pervades all nature **Allah** Mohammedan Supreme Being 1027 **Odin** Norse god of war and poetry **Mexitli** Indian goddess of the moon (Metztli)

Minding their voices peal through the crash of
    destruction,
Their brawny limbs passing safe over charred laths
    . . . . their white foreheads whole and unhurt out
    of the flames;
By the mechanic's wife with her babe at her nipple
    interceding for every person born;
Three scythes at harvest whizzing in a row from three
    lusty angels with shirts bagged out at their waists;
The snag-toothed hostler with red hair redeeming sins
    past and to come,   1040
Selling all he possesses and traveling on foot to fee
    lawyers for his brother and sit by him while he is
    tried for forgery;
What was strewn in the amplest strewing the square
    rod about me, and not filling the square rod then;
The bull and the bug never worshipped half enough,
Dung and dirt more admirable than was dreamed,
The supernatural of no account . . . . myself waiting
    my time to be one of the supremes,
The day getting ready for me when I shall do as much
    good as the best, and be as prodigious,
Guessing when I am it will not tickle me much to
    receive puffs out of pulpit or print;
By my life-lumps! becoming already a creator!
Putting myself here and now to the ambushed womb of
    the shadows!

[42] . . . . A call in the midst of the crowd,   1050
My own voice, orotund sweeping and final.

Come my children,
Come my boys and girls, and my women and household
    and intimates,

1043 **bull . . . bug** The bull was worshipped by ancient Egyptians, Assyrians, and the followers of Dionysus; the beetle, or scarab, was sacred in Egypt   1048 **life-lumps** humorous reference to phrenology   1051 **orotund** sonorous

70 Walt Whitman

Now the performer launches his nerve . . . . he has
passed his prelude on the reeds within.

Easily written loosefingered chords! I feel the thrum of
their climax and close.

My head evolves on my neck,
Music rolls, but not from the organ . . . . folks are
around me, but they are no household of mine.

Ever the hard and unsunk ground,
Ever the eaters and drinkers . . . . ever the upward
and downward sun . . . . ever the air and the
ceaseless tides,
Ever myself and my neighbors, refreshing and wicked
and real, 1060
Ever the old inexplicable query . . . . ever that
thorned thumb—that breath of itches and thirsts,
Ever the vexer's hoot! hoot! till we find where the sly
one hides and bring him forth;
Ever love . . . . ever the sobbing liquid of life,
Ever the bandage under the chin . . . . ever the
trestles of death.

Here and there with dimes on the eyes walking,
To feed the greed of the belly the brains liberally
spooning,
Tickets buying or taking or selling, but in to the feast
never once going;
Many sweating and ploughing and thrashing, and then
the chaff for payment receiving,
A few idly owning, and they the wheat continually
claiming.

This is the city . . . . and I am one of the citizens; 1070
Whatever interests the rest interests me . . . . politics,
churches, newspapers, schools,
Benevolent societies, improvements, banks, tariffs,
steamships, factories, markets,

1065 **dimes on the eyes** people blinded by their greed,
figuratively dead

Song of Myself   71

Stocks and stores and real estate and personal estate.

They who piddle and patter here in collars and tailed
   coats . . . . I am aware who they are . . . . and
   that they are not worms or fleas,
I acknowledge the duplicates of myself under all the
   scrape-lipped and pipe-legged concealments.

The weakest and shallowest is deathless with me,
What I do and say the same waits for them,
Every thought that flounders in me the same flounders
   in them.

I know perfectly well my own egotism,
And know my omnivorous words, and cannot say any
   less,   1080
And would fetch you whoever you are flush with myself.

My words are words of a questioning, and to
   indicate reality;
This printed and bound book . . . . but the printer
   and the printing-office boy?
The marriage estate and settlement . . . . but the
   body and mind of the bridegroom? also those of
   the bride?
The panorama of the sea . . . . but the sea itself?
The well-taken photographs . . . . but your wife or
   friend close and solid in your arms?
The fleet of ships of the line and all the modern
   improvements . . . . but the craft and pluck of the
   admiral?
The dishes and fare and furniture . . . . but the host
   and hostess, and the look out of their eyes?
The sky up there . . . . yet here or next door or
   across the way?
The saints and sages in history . . . . but you yourself?   1090
Sermons and creeds and theology . . . . but the human
   brain, and what is called reason, and what is called
   love, and what is called life?

72 *Walt Whitman*

[43] I do not despise your priests;
My faith is the greatest of faiths and the least of faiths,
Enclosing all worship ancient and modern, and all
  between ancient and modern,
Believing I shall come again upon the earth after five
  thousand years,
Waiting responses from oracles . . . . honoring the
  gods . . . . saluting the sun,
Making a fetish of the first rock or stump . . . .
  powowing with sticks in the circle of obis,
Helping the lama or brahmin as he trims the lamps of
  the idols,
Dancing yet through the streets in a phallic procession
  . . . . rapt and austere in the woods, a gymnosophist,
Drinking mead from the skull-cup . . . . to shasta and
  vedas admirant . . . . minding the koran,   1100
Walking the teokallis, spotted with gore from the stone
  and knife—beating the serpent-skin drum;
Accepting the gospels, accepting him that was crucified,
  knowing assuredly that he is divine,
To the mass kneeling—to the puritan's prayer rising—
  sitting patiently in a pew,
Ranting and frothing in my insane crisis—waiting
  dead-like till my spirit arouses me;
Looking forth on pavement and land, and outside of
  pavement and land,
Belonging to the winders of the circuit of circuits.

One of that centripetal and centrifugal gang,
I turn and talk like a man leaving charges before a
  journey.

1097 **fetish** worship of inanimate object **obis** *obeah,* sorcery of African origin   1098 **lama** priest of Tibetan Buddhism **brahmin** Hindu celebrant   1099 **phallic procession** early Greek worship of the male organ as the symbol of fertility **gymnosophist** sect of ancient Hindu philosophers who went naked 1100 **shasta and vedas** *shastra,* ancient scriptures of Hinduism **admirant** admiring (French)   1101 **teokallis** *teocalli,* ancient temple of Mexico

Down-hearted doubters, dull and excluded,
Frivolous sullen moping angry affected disheartened
    atheistical,
I know every one of you, and know the unspoken
    interrogatories,
By experience I know them.

How the flukes splash!
How they contort rapid as lightning, with spasms and
    spouts of blood!

Be at peace bloody flukes of doubters and sullen mopers,
I take my place among you as much as among any;
The past is the push of you and me and all precisely
    the same,
And the day and night are for you and me and all,
And what is yet untried and afterward is for you and
    me and all.

I do not know what is untried and afterward,
But I know it is sure and alive and sufficient.

Each who passes is considered, and each who stops is
    considered, and not a single one can it fail.

It cannot fail the young man who died and was buried,
Nor the young woman who died and was put by his side,
Nor the little child that peeped in at the door and
    then drew back and was never seen again,
Nor the old man who has lived without purpose, and
    feels it with bitterness worse than gall,
Nor him in the poorhouse tubercled by rum and the bad
    disorder,
Nor the numberless slaughtered and wrecked . . . .
    nor the brutish koboo, called the ordure of humanity,
Nor the sacs merely floating with open mouths for
    food to slip in,

1113 **flukes** whale's tail 1127 **tubercled** tubercular **bad disorder** venereal disease 1128 **koboo** apparently a wild tribe in folklore **ordure** excrement

74 *Walt Whitman*

Nor any thing in the earth, or down in the oldest
   graves of the earth,   1130
Nor any thing in the myriads of spheres, nor one of the
   myriads of myriads that inhabit them,
Nor the present, nor the least wisp that is known.

[44] It is time to explain myself . . . . let us stand up.

What is known I strip away . . . . I launch all men
   and women forward with me into the unknown.

The clock indicates the moment . . . . but what does
   eternity indicate?
Eternity lies in bottomless reservoirs . . . . its buckets
   are rising forever and ever,
They pour and they pour and they exhale away.

We have thus far exhausted trillions of winters and
   summers;
There are trillions ahead, and trillions ahead of them.

Births have brought us richness and variety,   1140
And other births will bring us richness and variety.

I do not call one greater and one smaller,
That which fills its period and place is equal to any.

Were mankind murderous or jealous upon you my
   brother or my sister?
I am sorry for you . . . . they are not murderous or
   jealous upon me;
All has been gentle with me . . . . I keep no account
   with lamentation;
What have I to do with lamentation?

I am an acme of things accomplished, and I am
   encloser of things to be.

My feet strike an apex of the apices of the stairs,

On every step bunches of ages, and larger bunches
    between the steps,
All below duly traveled—and still I mount and mount.

Rise after rise bow the phantoms behind me,
Afar down I see the huge first Nothing, the vapor
    from the nostrils of death,
I know I was even there .... I waited unseen and
    always,
And slept while God carried me through the lethargic
    mist,
And took my time .... and took no hurt from the
    fœtid carbon.

Long I was hugged close .... long and long.
Immense have been the preparations for me,
Faithful and friendly the arms that have helped me.

Cycles ferried my cradle, rowing and rowing like
    cheerful boatmen;
For room to me stars kept aside in their own rings,
They sent influences to look after what was to hold me.

Before I was born out of my mother generations guided
    me,
My embryo has never been torpid .... nothing
    could overlay it;
For it the nebula cohered to an orb .... the long
    slow strata piled to rest it on .... vast vegetables
    gave it sustenance,
Monstrous sauroids transported it in their mouths and
    deposited it with care.

All forces have been steadily employed to complete and
    delight me,
Now I stand on this spot with my soul.

1166 **sauroids** *Sauria*, prehistoric lizards

[45] Span of youth! Ever-pushed elasticity! Manhood balanced and florid and full!

My lovers suffocate me!
Crowding my lips, and thick in the pores of my skin,
Jostling me through streets and public halls . . . . coming naked to me at night,
Crying by day Ahoy from the rocks of the river . . . . swinging and chirping over my head,
Calling my name from flowerbeds or vines or tangled underbrush,
Or while I swim in the bath . . . . or drink from the pump at the corner . . . . or the curtain is down at the opera . . . . or I glimpse at a woman's face in the railroad car;
Lighting on every moment of my life,
Bussing my body with soft and balsamic busses,
Noiselessly passing handfuls out of their hearts and giving them to be mine.

Old age superbly rising! Ineffable grace of dying days!
Every condition promulges not only itself . . . . it promulges what grows after and out of itself,
And the dark hush promulges as much as any.

I open my scuttle at night and see the far-sprinkled systems,
And all I see, multiplied as high as I can cipher, edge but the rim of the farther systems.

Wider and wider they spread, expanding and always expanding,
Outward and outward and forever outward.

My sun has his sun, and round him obediently wheels,
He joins with his partners a group of superior circuit,
And greater sets follow, making specks of the greatest inside them.

1177 **Bussing** kissing 1180 **promulges** promulgates (archaic)
1182 **scuttle** opening with a lid in a building or ship

There is no stoppage, and never can be stoppage;
If I and you and the worlds and all beneath or upon
 their surfaces, and all the palpable life, were this
 moment reduced back to a pallid float, it would not
 avail in the long run, 1190
We should surely bring up again where we now stand,
And as surely go as much farther, and then farther
 and farther.

A few quadrillions of eras, a few octillions of cubic
 leagues, do not hazard the span, or make it
 impatient,
They are but parts . . . . any thing is but a part.

See ever so far . . . . there is limitless space outside of
 that,
Count ever so much . . . . there is limitless time
 around that.

Our rendezvous is fitly appointed . . . . God will be
 there and wait till we come.

[46] I know I have the best of time and space—and that I
 was never measured, and never will be measured.

I tramp a perpetual journey,
My signs are a rain-proof coat and good shoes and a
 staff cut from the woods; 1200
No friend of mine takes his ease in my chair,
I have no chair, nor church nor philosophy;
I lead no man to a dinner-table or library or exchange,
But each man and each woman of you I lead upon a
 knoll,
My left hand hooks you round the waist,
My right hand points to landscapes of continents,
 and a plain public road.

Not I, not any one else can travel that road for you,
You must travel it for yourself.

It is not far . . . . it is within reach,
Perhaps you have been on it since you were born, and
   did not know,
Perhaps it is every where on water and on land.

Shoulder your duds, and I will mine, and let us
   hasten forth;
Wonderful cities and free nations we shall fetch as we go.

If you tire, give me both burdens, and rest the chuff of
   your hand on my hip,
And in due time you shall repay the same service to me;
For after we start we never lie by again.

This day before dawn I ascended a hill and looked at
   the crowded heaven,
And I said to my spirit, When we become the enfolders
   of those orbs and the pleasure and knowledge of
   every thing in them, shall we be filled and satisfied
   then?
And my spirit said No, we level that lift to pass and
   continue beyond.

You are also asking me questions, and I hear you;
I answer that I cannot answer . . . . you must find
   out for yourself.

Sit awhile wayfarer,
Here are biscuits to eat and here is milk to drink,
But as soon as you sleep and renew yourself in sweet
   clothes I will certainly kiss you with my goodbye kiss
   and open the gate for your egress hence.

Long enough have you dreamed contemptible dreams,
Now I wash the gum from your eyes,
You must habit yourself to the dazzle of the light and
   of every moment of your life.

Long have you timidly waded, holding a plank by the
   shore,
Now I will you to be a bold swimmer,

1214 **chuff** chubby or fat part of the hand (dialectal)

To jump off in the midst of the sea, and rise again and
    nod to me and shout, and laughingly dash with
    your hair.   1230

[47] I am the teacher of athletes,
He that by me spreads a wider breast than my own
    proves the width of my own,
He most honors my style who learns under it to destroy
    the teacher.

The boy I love, the same becomes a man not through
    derived power but in his own right,
Wicked, rather than virtuous out of conformity or fear,
Fond of his sweetheart, relishing well his steak,
Unrequited love or a slight cutting him worse than a
    wound cuts,
First rate to ride, to fight, to hit the bull's eye, to sail a
    skiff, to sing a song or play on the banjo,
Preferring scars and faces pitted with smallpox over all
    latherers and those that keep out of the sun.

I teach straying from me, yet who can stray from me?   1240
I follow you whoever you are from the present hour;
My words itch at your ears till you understand them.

I do not say these things for a dollar, or to fill up the
    time while I wait for a boat;
It is you talking just as much as myself . . . . I act as
    the tongue of you,
It was tied in your mouth . . . . in mine it begins to be
    loosened.

I swear I will never mention love or death inside a
    house,
And I swear I never will translate myself at all, only to
    him or her who privately stays with me in the open air.

If you would understand me go to the heights or
    water-shore,
The nearest gnat is an explanation and a drop or the
    motion of waves a key,

The maul the oar and the handsaw second my words. 1250

No shuttered room or school can commune with me,
But roughs and little children better than they.

The young mechanic is closest to me . . . . he knows me pretty well,
The woodman that takes his axe and jug with him shall take me with him all day,
The farmboy ploughing in the field feels good at the sound of my voice,
In vessels that sail my words must sail . . . . I go with fishermen and seamen, and love them,
My face rubs to the hunter's face when he lies down alone in his blanket,
The driver thinking of me does not mind the jolt of his wagon,
The young mother and old mother shall comprehend me,
The girl and the wife rest the needle a moment and forget where they are, 1260
They and all would resume what I have told them.

[48] I have said that the soul is not more than the body,
And I have said that the body is not more than the soul,
And nothing, not God, is greater to one than one's-self is,
And whoever walks a furlong without sympathy walks to his own funeral, dressed in his shroud,
And I or you pocketless of a dime may purchase the pick of the earth,
And to glance with an eye or show a bean in its pod confounds the learning of all times,
And there is no trade or employment but the young man following it may become a hero,
And there is no object so soft but it makes a hub for the wheeled universe,
And any man or woman shall stand cool and supercilious before a million universes. 1270

And I call to mankind, Be not curious about God,

For I who am curious about each am not curious about
  God,
No array of terms can say how much I am at peace
  about God and about death.

I hear and behold God in every object, yet I understand
  God not in the least,
Nor do I understand who there can be more wonderful
  than myself.

Why should I wish to see God better than this day?
I see something of God each hour of the twenty-four,
  and each moment then,
In the faces of men and women I see God, and in my
  own face in the glass;
I find letters from God dropped in the street, and
  every one is signed by God's name,
And I leave them where they are, for I know that
  others will punctually come forever and ever.   1280

[49] And as to you death, and you bitter hug of mortality
  . . . . it is idle to try to alarm me.

To his work without flinching the accoucheur comes,
I see the elderhand pressing receiving supporting,
I recline by the sills of the exquisite flexible doors
  . . . . and mark the outlet, and mark the relief
  and escape.
And as to you corpse I think you are good manure,
  but that does not offend me,
I smell the white roses sweetscented and growing,
I reach to the leafy lips . . . . I reach to the polished
  breasts of melons,

And as to you life, I reckon you are the leavings of
  many deaths,
No doubt I have died myself ten thousand times
  before.

1282 **accoucheur** obstetrician (French)

I hear you whispering there O stars of heaven,
O suns .... O grass of graves .... O perpetual
 transfers and promotions .... if you do not say
 anything how can I say anything?

Of the turbid pool that lies in the autumn forest,
Of the moon that descends the steeps of the soughing
 twilight,
Toss, sparkles of day and dusk .... toss on the
 black stems that decay in the muck,
Toss to the moaning gibberish of the dry limbs.

I ascend from the moon .... I ascend from the
 night,
And perceive of the ghastly glitter the sunbeams
 reflected,
And debouch to the steady and central from the
 offspring great or small.

[50] There is that in me .... I do not know what it is
 .... but I know it is in me.

Wrenched and sweaty .... calm and cool then my
 body becomes;
I sleep .... I sleep long.

I do not know it .... it is without name ....
 it is a word unsaid,
It is not in any dictionary or utterance or symbol.

Something it swings on more than the earth I swing
 on,
To it the creation is the friend whose embracing
 awakes me.
Perhaps I might tell more .... Outlines! I plead
 for my brothers and sisters.

Do you see O my brothers and sisters?
It is not chaos or death .... it is form and union

1298 **debouch** emerge

and plan . . . . it is eternal life . . . . it is happiness.

[51] The past and present wilt . . . . I have filled them and emptied them,
And proceed to fill my next fold of the future.

Listener up there! Here you . . . . what have you to confide to me?
Look in my face while I snuff the sidle of evening,
Talk honestly, for no one else hears you, and I stay only a minute longer.

Do I contradict myself?
Very well then . . . . I contradict myself;
I am large . . . . I contain multitudes.

I concentrate toward them that are nigh . . . . I wait on the door-slab.

Who has done his day's work and will soonest be through with his supper?
Who wishes to walk with me?

Will you speak before I am gone? Will you prove already too late?

[52] The spotted hawk swoops by and accuses me . . . . he complains of my gab and my loitering.

I too am not a bit tamed . . . . I too am untranslatable,
I sound my barbaric yawp over the roofs of the world.

The last scud of day holds back for me,
It flings my likeness after the rest and true as any on the shadowed wilds,
It coaxes me to the vapor and the dusk.

1312 **snuff the sidle** extinguish the oblique light of the evening
1324 **scud** vapory clouds

84 Walt Whitman

I depart as air . . . . I shake my white locks at the
   runaway sun,
I effuse my flesh in eddies and drift it in lacy jags.

I bequeath myself to the dirt to grow from the grass
   I love,
If you want me again look for me under your bootsoles.   1330

You will hardly know who I am or what I mean,
But I shall be good health to you nevertheless,
And filter and fibre your blood.

Failing to fetch me at first keep encouraged,
Missing me one place search another,
I stop some where waiting for you

1328 **effuse** pour out   1336 **you** the omission of the period in the 1855 edition may have been accidental or intended, as recently suggested, to indicate eternal recurrence

Crossing Brooklyn Ferry

[1] Flood-tide below me! I watch you, face to face;
Clouds of the west! sun there half an hour high! I see
you also face to face.

Crowds of men and women attired in the usual
costumes! how curious you are to me!
On the ferry-boats, the hundreds and hundreds that
cross, returning home, are more curious to me than
you suppose,
And you that shall cross from shore to shore years
hence, are more to me, and more in my meditations,
than you might suppose.

[2] The impalpable sustenance of me from all things, at
all hours of the day,
The simple, compact, well-joined scheme—myself
disintegrated, every one disintegrated, yet part of
the scheme,
The similitudes of the past, and those of the future,
The glories strung like beads on my smallest sights and
hearings—on the walk in the street, and the passage
over the river,
The current rushing so swiftly, and swimming with
me far away,
The others that are to follow me, the ties between me
and them,
The certainty of others—the life, love, sight, hearing
of others.

The poem appeared first in 1856 as "Sun-Down Poem." The
following lines were dropped in 1881: ll. 22, 51, 95–99, 109,
and 137–140. Two excisions were made in 1871: ll. 115 and
118

86 *Walt Whitman*

Others will enter the gates of the ferry, and cross
   from shore to shore,
Others will watch the run of the flood-tide,
Others will see the shipping of Manhattan north and
   west, and the heights of Brooklyn to the south
   and east,
Others will see the islands large and small,
Fifty years hence, others will see them as they cross,
   the sun half an hour high,
A hundred years hence, or ever so many hundred years
   hence, others will see them,
Will enjoy the sunset, the pouring in of the flood-tide,
   the falling back to the sea of the ebb-tide.

[3] It avails not, neither time or place—distance avails not,   20
I am with you, you men and women of a generation,
   or ever so many generations hence,
I project myself—also I return—I am with you, and
   know how it is.

Just as you feel when you look on the river and sky,
   so I felt,
Just as any of you is one of a living crowd, I was one
   of a crowd,
Just as you are refreshed by the gladness of the river,
   and the bright flow, I was refreshed,
Just as you stand and lean on the rail, yet hurry with
   the swift current, I stood, yet was hurried,
Just as you look on the numberless masts of ships,
   and the thick-stemmed pipes of steamboats, I
   looked.

I too many and many a time crossed the river, the sun
   half an hour high,
I watched the Twelfth Month sea-gulls—I saw them
   high in the air, floating with motionless wings,
   oscillating their bodies,
I saw how the glistening yellow lit up parts of their
   bodies, and left the rest in strong shadow,   30
I saw the slow-wheeling circles, and the gradual edging
   toward the south.

Crossing Brooklyn Ferry 87

I too saw the reflection of the summer sky in the
  water,
Had my eyes dazzled by the shimmering track of beams,
Looked at the fine centrifugal spokes of light round
  the shape of my head in the sun-lit water,
Looked on the haze on the hills southward and
  southwestward,
Looked on the vapor as it flew in fleeces tinged with
  violet,
Looked toward the lower bay to notice the arriving
  ships,
Saw their approach, saw aboard those that were near
  me,
Saw the white sails of schooners and sloops, saw the
  ships at anchor,
The sailors at work in the rigging, or out astride the
  spars,   40
The round masts, the swinging motion of the hulls,
  the slender serpentine pennants,
The large and small steamers in motion, the pilots in
  their pilot-houses,
The white wake left by the passage, the quick
  tremulous whirl of the wheels,
The flags of all nations, the falling of them at sun-set,
The scallop-edged waves in the twilight, the ladled
  cups, the frolicsome crests and glistening,
The stretch afar growing dimmer and dimmer, the
  gray walls of the granite store-houses by the docks,
On the river the shadowy group, the big steam-tug
  closely flanked on each side by the barges—the
  hay-boat, the belated lighter,
On the neighboring shore, the fires from the foundry
  chimneys burning high and glaringly into the
  night,
Casting their flicker of black, contrasted with wild red
  and yellow light, over the tops of houses,
  and down into the clefts of streets.

[4] These, and all else, were to me the same as they are
      to you,   50
    I project myself a moment to tell you—also I return.

I loved well those cities,
I loved well the stately and rapid river,
The men and women I saw were all near to me,
Others the same—others who look back on me,
 because I looked forward to them,
(The time will come, though I stop here to-day and
 to-night.)

[5] What is it, then, between us?
What is the count of the scores or hundreds of years
 between us?

Whatever it is, it avails not—distance avails not, and
 place avails not.

I too lived, (I was of old Brooklyn,) 60
I too walked the streets of Manhattan Island, and
 bathed in the waters around it,
I too felt the curious abrupt questionings stir within
 me,
In the day, among crowds of people, sometimes they
 came upon me,
In my walks home late at night, or as I lay in my
 bed, they came upon me.

I too had been struck from the float forever held in
 solution,
I too had received identity by my body,
That I was, I knew was of my body—and what I
 should be, I knew I should be of my body.

[6] It is not upon you alone the dark patches fall,
The dark threw patches down upon me also,
The best I had done seemed to me blank and
 suspicious,
My great thoughts, as I supposed them, were they not
 in reality meagre? would not people laugh at me? 70

Crossing Brooklyn Ferry

It is not you alone who know what it is to be evil,
I am he who knew what it was to be evil,
I too knitted the old knot of contrariety,
Blabbed, blushed, resented, lied, stole, grudged,
Had guile, anger, lust, hot wishes I dared not speak,
Was wayward, vain, greedy, shallow, sly, cowardly,
    malignant,
The wolf, the snake, the hog, not wanting in me,
The cheating look, the frivolous word, the adulterous
    wish, not wanting,
Refusals, hates, postponements, meanness, laziness,
    none of these wanting.   80

But I was a Manhattanese, free, friendly, and proud!
I was called by my nighest name by clear loud voices
    of young men as they saw me approaching or
    passing,
Felt their arms on my neck as I stood, or the negligent
    leaning of their flesh against me as I sat,
Saw many I loved in the street, or ferry-boat, or public
    assembly, yet never told them a word,
Lived the same life with the rest, the same old
    laughing, gnawing, sleeping,
Played the part that still looks back on the actor or
    actress,
The same old rôle, the rôle that is what we make it,
    as great as we like,
Or as small as we like, or both great and small.

[7] Closer yet I approach you,
    What thought you have of me, I had as much of you
        —I laid in my stores in advance,   90
    I considered long and seriously of you before you
        were born.
    Who was to know what should come home to me?
    Who knows but I am enjoying this?
    Who knows but I am as good as looking at you now,
        for all you cannot see me?

90 Walt Whitman

It is not you alone, nor I alone,
Not a few races, nor a few generations, nor a few
 centuries,
It is that each came, or comes, or shall come, from its
 due emission, without fail, either now, or then, or
 henceforth.

Every thing indicates—the smallest does, and the
 largest does,
A necessary film envelops all, and envelops the Soul
 for a proper time.

[8] Now I am curious what sight can ever be more stately
 and admirable to me than my mast-hemm'd
 Manhatta,
My river and sun-set, and my scallop-edged waves of
 flood-tide,
The sea-gulls oscillating their bodies, the hay-boat in
 the twilight, and the belated lighter;
Curious what Gods can exceed these that clasp me by
 the hand, and with voices I love call me promptly
 and loudly by my nighest name as I approach,
Curious what is more subtle than this which ties me
 to the woman or man that looks in my face,
Which fuses me into you now, and pours my meaning
 into you.
We understand, then, do we not?
What I promised without mentioning it, have you not
 accepted?
What the study could not teach—what the preaching
 could not accomplish is accomplished, is it not?
What the push of reading could not start is started by me
 personally, is it not?

[9] Flow on, river! flow with the flood-tide, and ebb with
 the ebb-tide!
Frolic on, crested and scallop-edged waves!
Gorgeous clouds of the sun-set! drench with your
 splendor me, or the men and women generations
 after me;

Crossing Brooklyn Ferry

Cross from shore to shore, countless crowds of passengers!
Stand up, tall masts of Mannahatta!—stand up, beautiful hills of Brooklyn!
Bully for you! you proud, friendly, free Manhattanese!
Throb, baffled and curious brain! throw out questions and answers!
Suspend here and everywhere, eternal float of solution!
Blab, blush, lie, steal, you or I or any one after us!
Gaze, loving and thirsting eyes, in the house, or street, or public assembly!
Sound out, voices of young men! loudly and musically call me by my nighest name!
Live, old life! play the part that looks back on the actor or actress!
Play the old rôle, the rôle that is great or small, according as one makes it!
Consider, you who peruse me, whether I may not in unknown ways be looking upon you;
Be firm, rail over the river, to support those who lean idly, yet haste with the hasting current;
Fly on, sea-birds! fly sideways, or wheel in large circles high in the air;
Receive the summer-sky, you water! and faithfully hold it, till all downcast eyes have time to take it from you;
Diverge, fine spokes of light, from the shape of my head, or any one's head, in the sun-lit water;
Come on, ships from the lower bay! pass up or down, white-sailed schooners, sloops, lighters!
Flaunt away, flags of all nations! be duly lowered at sun-set;
Burn high your fires, foundry chimneys! cast black shadows at nightfall! cast red and yellow light over the tops of the houses;
Appearances, now or henceforth, indicate what you are;
You necessary film, continue to envelop the Soul;
About my body for me, and your body for you, be hung our divinest aromas;

92 Walt Whitman

Thrive, cities! bring your freight, bring your shows,
    ample and sufficient rivers;
Expand, being than which none else is perhaps more
    spiritual;
Keep your places, objects than which none else is
    more lasting.

We descend upon you and all things—we arrest you
    all,
We realize the Soul only by you, you faithful solids
    and fluids,
Through you color, form, location, sublimity, ideality,
Through you every proof, comparison, and all the
    suggestions and determinations of ourselves. 140

You have waited, you always wait, you dumb,
    beautiful ministers! you novices!
We receive you with free sense at last, and are
    insatiate henceforward,
Not you any more shall be able to foil us, or withhold
    yourselves from us,
We use you, and do not cast you aside—we plant
    you permanently within us,
We fathom you not—we love you—there is perfection
    in you also,
You furnish your parts toward eternity,
Great or small, you furnish your parts toward the
    Soul.

As I Ebb'd with the Ocean of Life

[1] Elemental drifts!
O I wish I could impress others as you and the waves have just been impressing me.

As I ebbed with an ebb of the ocean of life,
As I wended the shores I know,
As I walked where the sea-ripples wash you, Paumanok,
Where they rustle up, hoarse and sibilant,
Where the fierce old mother endlessly cries for her castaways,
I, musing, late in the autumn day, gazing off southward,
Alone, held by the eternal self of me that threatens to get the better of me, and stifle me,
Was seized by the spirit that trails in the lines underfoot,   10
In the rim, the sediment, that stands for all the water and all the land of the globe.

Fascinated, my eyes, reverting from the south, dropped, to follow those slender winrows,
Chaff, straw, splinters of wood, weeds, and the sea-gluten,
Scum, scales from shining rocks, leaves of salt-lettuce, left by the tide;

This poem was first published as "Bardic Symbols" in *The Atlantic Monthly*, April, 1860; the editor, James Russell Lowell, insisted upon the removal of ll. 68–69, which were restored in the third edition of *Leaves of Grass*. Whitman excised ll. 1–2 in 1881, ll. 41, and 56–58 in 1867   5 **Paumanok** Indian name for Long Island, Whitman's birthplace   12 **winrows** banks or ridges   13 **sea-gluten** sticky substance   14 **salt-lettuce** seaweed

Miles walking, the sound of breaking waves the other
    side of me,
Paumanok, there and then, as I thought the old
    thought of likenesses,
These you presented to me, you fish-shaped island,
As I wended the shores I know,
As I walked with that eternal self of me, seeking types.

[2] As I wend the shores I know not,
    As I listen to the dirge, the voices of men and women
        wrecked,
    As I inhale the impalpable breezes that set in upon me,
    As the ocean so mysterious rolls toward me closer and
        closer,
    At once I find, the least thing that belongs to me, or
        that I see or touch, I know not;
    I, too, but signify, at the utmost, a little washed-up
        drift,
    A few sands and dead leaves to gather,
    Gather, and merge myself as part of the sands and drift.

O baffled, balked,
Bent to the very earth, here preceding what follows,
Oppressed with myself that I have dared to open my
    mouth,
Aware now, that, amid all the blab whose echoes
    recoil upon me, I have not once had the least idea
    who or what I am,
But that before all my insolent poems the real M*E*
    still stands untouched, untold, altogether unreached,
Withdrawn far, mocking me with mock-congratulatory
    signs and bows,
With peals of distant ironical laughter at every word I
    have written or shall write,
Striking me with insults till I fall helpless upon the sand.

O I perceive I have not understood anything—not a
    single object—and that no man ever can.

I perceive Nature here, in sight of the sea, is taking
    advantage of me, to dart upon me, and sting me,

Because I was assuming so much,
And because I have dared to open my mouth to sing
    at all.

[3] You oceans both! You tangible land! Nature!   40
Be not too rough with me—I submit—I close with you,
These little shreds shall, indeed, stand for all.

You friable shore, with trails of debris!
You fish-shaped island! I take what is underfoot;
What is yours is mine, my father.

I too Paumanok,
I too have bubbled up, floated the measureless float,
    and been washed on your shores;
I too am but a trail of drift and debris,
I too leave little wrecks upon you, you fish-shaped island.

I throw myself upon your breast, my father,   50
I cling to you so that you cannot unloose me,
I hold you so firm, till you answer me something.

Kiss me, my father,
Touch me with your lips, as I touch those I love,
Breathe to me, while I hold you close, the secret of the
    wondrous murmuring I envy,
For I fear I shall become crazed, if I cannot emulate it,
    and utter myself as well as it.

Sea-raff! Crook-tongued waves!
O, I will yet sing, some day, what you have said to me.

[4] Ebb, ocean of life, (the flow will return,)
Cease not your moaning, you fierce old mother,   60
Endlessly cry for your castaways—but fear not, deny not
    me,
Rustle not up so hoarse and angry against my feet, as
    I touch you, or gather from you.

43 **friable** easily pulverized   57 **Sea-raff** debris

I mean tenderly by you,
I gather for myself, and for this phantom, looking down
    where we lead, and following me and mine.

Me and mine!
We, loose winrows, little corpses,
Froth, snowy white, and bubbles,
(See! from my dead lips the ooze exuding at last!
See—the prismatic colors, glistening and rolling!)
Tufts of straw, sands, fragments, 70
Buoyed hither from many moods, one contradicting
    another,
From the storm, the long calm, the darkness, the swell,
Musing, pondering, a breath, a briny tear, a dab of
    liquid or soil,
Up just as much out of fathomless workings fermented
    and thrown,
A limp blossom or two, torn, just as much over waves
    floating, drifted at random,
Just as much for us that sobbing dirge of Nature,
Just as much, whence we come, that blare of the
    cloud-trumpets;
We, capricious, brought hither, we know not whence,
    spread out before You, up there, walking or sitting,
Whoever you are—we too lie in drifts at your feet.

from Children of Adam

To the Garden the World

To the garden, the world, anew ascending,
Potent mates, daughters, sons, preluding,
The love, the life of their bodies, meaning and being,
Curious, here behold my resurrection, after slumber,
The revolving cycles, in their wide sweep, having brought
    me again,
Amorous, mature—all beautiful to me—all wondrous,
My limbs, and the quivering fire that ever plays through
    them, for reasons, most wondrous;
Existing, I peer and penetrate still,
Content with the present—content with the past,
By my side, or back of me, Eve following,   10
Or in front, and I following her just the same.

The poems in this group were intended to describe "amativeness," a phrenological term meaning love of women. The "Calamus" poems were to illustrate "adhesiveness," another phrenological term signifying male friendship. "Children of Adam" includes, as the notes indicate, a number of poems which had appeared before 1860

From Pent-up Aching Rivers

From that of myself, without which I were nothing,
From what I am determined to make illustrious, even
    if I stand sole among men,

The title comes from the first line which was added in 1867. The following excisions were made: ll. 15–16 in 1881, l. 26 in 1871, and ll. 44–45 in 1881

From my own voice resonant—singing the phallus,
Singing the song of procreation,
Singing the need of superb children, and therein superb
    grown people,
Singing the muscular urge and the blending,
Singing the bedfellow's song, (O resistless yearning!
O for any and each, the body correlative attracting!
O for you, whoever you are, your correlative body!
    O it, more than all else, you delighting!)
From the pent up rivers of myself,   10
From the hungry gnaw that eats me night and day,
From native moments—from bashful pains—singing
    them,
Singing something yet unfound, though I have diligently
    sought it, ten thousand years,
Singing the true song of the Soul, fitful, at random,
Singing what, to the Soul, entirely redeemed her, the
    faithful one, the prostitute, who detained me when
    I went to the city,
Singing the song of prostitutes;
Renascent with grossest Nature, among animals,
Or that—of them, and what goes with them, my poems
    informing,
Of the smell of apples and lemons—of the pairing of
    birds,
Of the wet of woods—of the lapping of waves,   20
Of the mad pushes of waves upon the land—I them
    chanting,
The overture lightly sounding—the strain anticipating,
The welcome nearness—the sight of the perfect body,
The swimmer swimming naked in the bath, or motionless
    on his back lying and floating,
The female form approaching—I, pensive, love-flesh
    tremulous, aching;
The slave's body for sale—I, sternly, with harsh voice,
    auctioneering,
The divine list, for myself or you, or for any one, making,
The face—the limbs—the index from head to foot,
    and what it arouses,
The mystic deliria—the madness amorous—the utter
    abandonment,

Children of Adam

(Hark, close and still, what I now whisper to you,
I love you—O you entirely possess me,
O I wish that you and I escape from the rest, and go
    utterly off—O free and lawless,
Two hawks in the air—two fishes swimming in the sea
    not more lawless than we;)
The furious storm through me careering—I passionately
    trembling,
The oath of the inseparableness of two together—of the
    woman that loves me, and whom I love more than
    my life—That oath swearing,
(O I willingly stake all, for you!
O let me be lost, if it must be so!
O you and I—what is it to us what the rest do or think?
What is all else to us? only that we enjoy each other,
    and exhaust each other, if it must be so;)
From the master—the pilot I yield the vessel to,
The general commanding me, commanding all—from
    him permission taking,
From time the programme hastening, (I have loitered
    too long, as it is;)
From sex—From the warp and from the woof,
(To talk to the perfect girl who understands me—the
    girl of The States,
To waft to her these from my own lips—to effuse them
    from my own body;)
From privacy—From frequent repinings alone,
From plenty of persons near, and yet the right person
    not near,
From the soft sliding of hands over me, and thrusting
    of fingers through my hair and beard,
From the long-sustained kiss upon the mouth or bosom,
From the close pressure that makes me or any man
    drunk, fainting with excess,
From what the divine husband knows—from the work
    of fatherhood,
From exultation, victory, and relief—from the bedfellow's
    embrace in the night,
From the act-poems of eyes, hands, hips, and bosoms,
From the cling of the trembling arm,
From the bending curve and the clinch,

100   Walt Whitman

From side by side, the pliant coverlid off throwing,
From the one so unwilling to have me leave—and
    me just as unwilling to leave,
(Yet a moment, O tender waiter, and I return,)
From the hour of shining stars and dropping dews,
From the night, a moment, I, emerging, flitting out,   60
Celebrate you, enfans prepared for,
And you, stalwart loins.

A Woman Waits for Me

A woman waits for me—she contains all, nothing is
    lacking,
Yet all were lacking, if sex were lacking, or if the
    moisture of the right man were lacking.

Sex contains all,
Bodies, Souls, meanings, proofs, purities, delicacies,
    results, promulgations,
Songs, commands, health, pride, the maternal mystery,
    the semitic milk,
All hopes, benefactions, bestowals,
All the passions, loves, beauties, delights of the earth,
All the governments, judges, gods, followed persons of
    the earth,
These are contained in sex, as parts of itself, and
    justifications of itself.

Without shame the man I like knows and avows the
    deliciousness of his sex,   10
Without shame the woman I like knows and avows hers.
O I will fetch bully breeds of children yet!
I will dismiss myself from impassive women,
I will go stay with her who waits for me, and with
    those women that are warm-blooded and sufficient
    for me;

61 **enfans** children (French)
Entitled "Poem of Procreation" in 1856. Line 12 was deleted in
1867   5 **semitic** later altered to seminal

Children of Adam

I see that they understand me, and do not deny me,
I see that they are worthy of me—I will be the robust
  husband of those women.

They are not one jot less than I am,
They are tanned in the face by shining suns and blowing
  winds,
Their flesh has the old divine suppleness and strength,
They know how to swim, row, ride, wrestle, shoot,
  run, strike, retreat, advance, resist, defend themselves,
They are ultimate in their own right—they are calm,
  clear, well-possessed of themselves.

I draw you close to me, you women!
I cannot let you go, I would do you good,
I am for you, and you are for me, not only for our own
  sake, but for others' sakes;
Enveloped in you sleep greater heroes and bards,
They refuse to awake at the touch of any man but me.

It is I, you women—I make my way,
I am stern, acrid, large, undissuadable—but I love you,
I do not hurt you any more than is necessary for you,
I pour the stuff to start sons and daughters fit for These
  States—I press with slow rude muscle,
I brace myself effectually—I listen to no entreaties,
I dare not withdraw till I deposit what has so long
  accumulated within me.

Through you I drain the pent-up rivers of myself,
In you I wrap a thousand onward years,
On you I graft the grafts of the best-beloved of me and
  of America,
The drops I distil upon you shall grow fierce and athletic
  girls, new artists, musicians, and singers,
The babes I beget upon you are to beget babes in their
  turn,
I shall demand perfect men and women out of my
  love-spendings,
I shall expect them to interpenetrate with others, as I
  and you interpenetrate now,

I shall count on the fruits of the gushing showers of
    them, as I count on the fruits of the gushing showers
    I give now,
I shall look for loving crops from the birth, life, death,
    immortality, I plant so lovingly now.

Spontaneous Me

Spontaneous me, Nature,
The loving day, the friend I am happy with,
The arm of my friend hanging idly over my shoulder,
The hill-side whitened with blossoms of the mountain
    ash,
The same, late in autumn—the gorgeous hues of red,
    yellow, drab, purple, and light and dark green,
The rich coverlid of the grass—animals and birds—the
    private untrimmed bank—the primitive apples—the
    pebble-stones,
Beautiful dripping fragments—the negligent list of one
    after another, as I happen to call them to me, or
    think of them,
The real poems, (what we call poems being merely
    pictures,)
The poems of the privacy of the night, and of men
    like me,
This poem, drooping shy and unseen, that I always
    carry, and that all men carry,
(Know, once for all, avowed on purpose, wherever are
    men like me, are our lusty, lurking, masculine,
    poems,)
Love-thoughts, love-juice, love-odor, love-yielding,
    love-climbers, and the climbing sap,
Arms and hands of love—lips of love—phallic thumb
    of love—breasts of love—bellies pressed and glued
    together with love,

Called "Bunch Poem" in 1856, a title more descriptive of its
sexual content than the present one

Children of Adam

Earth of chaste love—life that is only life after love,
The body of my love—the body of the woman I love—
    the body of the man—the body of the earth,
Soft forenoon airs that blow from the south-west,
The hairy wild-bee that murmurs and hankers up and
    down—that gripes the full-grown lady-flower, curves
    upon her with amorous firm legs, takes his will of her,
    and holds himself tremulous and tight upon her till
    he is satisfied,
The wet of woods through the early hours,
Two sleepers at night lying close together as they sleep,
    one with an arm slanting down across and below the
    waist of the other,
The smell of apples, aromas from crushed sage-plant,
    mint, birch-bark,
The boy's longings, the glow and pressure as he confides
    to me what he was dreaming,
The dead leaf whirling its spiral whirl, and falling still
    and content to the ground,
The no-formed stings that sights, people, objects, sting
    me with,
The hubbed sting of myself, stinging me as much as it
    ever can any one,
The sensitive, orbic, underlapped brothers, that only
    privileged feelers may be intimate where they are,
The curious roamer, the hand, roaming all over the body
    —the bashful withdrawing of flesh where the fingers
    soothingly pause and edge themselves,
The limpid liquid within the young man,
The vexed corrosion, so pensive and so painful,
The torment—the irritable tide that will not be at rest,
The like of the same I feel—the like of the same in others,
The young woman that flushes and flushes, and the
    young man that flushes and flushes,
The young man that wakes, deep at night, the hot hand
    seeking to repress what would master him—the strange
    half-welcome pangs, visions, sweats,
The pulse pounding through palms and trembling
    encircling fingers—the young man all colored, red,
    ashamed, angry;

25 **brothers** genitals

The souse upon me of my lover the sea, as I lie willing
    and naked,
The merriment of the twin-babes that crawl over the grass
    in the sun, the mother never turning her vigilant
    eyes from them,
The walnut-trunk, the walnut-husks, and the ripening or
    ripened long-round walnuts,
The continence of vegetables, birds, animals,
The consequent meanness of me should I skulk or find
    myself indecent, while birds and animals never once
    skulk or find themselves indecent,
The great chastity of paternity, to match the great chastity
    of maternity,
The oath of procreation I have sworn—my Adamic
    and fresh daughters, 40
The greed that eats me day and night with hungry gnaw,
    till I saturate what shall produce boys to fill my place
    when I am through,
The wholesome relief, repose, content,
And this bunch plucked at random from myself,
It has done its work—I toss it carelessly to fall where
    it may.

Native Moments

Native moments! when you come upon me—Ah you are
    here now!
Give me now libidinous joys only!
Give me the drench of my passions! Give me life coarse
    and rank!
To-day, I go consort with nature's darlings—to-night too,
I am for those who believe in loose delights—I share
    the midnight orgies of young men,
I dance with the dancers, and drink with the drinkers,
The echoes ring with our indecent calls,

I take for my love some prostitute—I pick out some
 low person for my dearest friend,
He shall be lawless, rude, illiterate—he shall be one
 condemned by others for deeds done;
I will play a part no longer—Why should I exile myself
 from my companions?
O you shunned persons! I at least do not shun you,
I come forthwith in your midst—I will be your poet,
I will be more to you than to any of the rest.

Once I Pass'd through a Populous City

Once I passed through a populous city, imprinting my
 brain, for future use, with its shows, architecture,
 customs, and traditions;
Yet now, of all that city, I remember only a woman
 I casually met there, who detained me for love of me,
Day by day and night by night we were together,—
 All else has long been forgotten by me,
I remember I say only that woman who passionately
 clung to me,
Again we wander—we love—we separate again,
Again she holds me by the hand—I must not go!
I see her close beside me, with silent lips, sad and
 tremulous.

8 The first half of line 8 was excised in 1881
2 The manuscript version of this line reads: "But now of all
that city I remember only the man who wandered with me,
there, for love of me" 4 The manuscript reading (in part)
is: "—I remember, I say, only one rude and ignorant man"

from Calamus

In Paths Untrodden

In paths untrodden,
In the growth by margins of pond-waters,
Escaped from the life that exhibits itself,
From all the standards hitherto published—from the
 pleasures, profits, conformities,
Which too long I was offering to feed to my Soul;
Clear to me now, standards not yet published—clear to
 me that my Soul,
That the Soul of the man I speak for, feeds, rejoices
 only in comrades;
Here, by myself, away from the clank of the world,
Tallying and talked to here by tongues aromatic,
No longer abashed—for in this secluded spot I can
 respond as I would not dare elsewhere,   10
Strong upon me the life that does not exhibit itself,
 yet contains all the rest,
Resolved to sing no songs to-day but those of manly
 attachment,
Projecting them along that substantial life,
Bequeathing, hence, types of athletic love,
Afternoon, this delicious Ninth Month, in my forty-first
 year,
I proceed, for all who are, or have been, young men,
To tell the secret of my nights and days,
To celebrate the need of comrades.

Whitman defined his symbol in 1867: " 'Calamus' . . . is the very large & aromatic grass, or rush, growing about water-ponds in the valleys . . . The recherché or ethereal sense of the term . . . arises probably from the actual Calamus presenting the biggest & hardiest kind of spears of grass—and their fresh, aquatic, pungent bouquet." 15 **Ninth Month** September 1859; also a birth symbol

Scented Herbage of My Breast

Scented herbage of my breast,
Leaves from you I yield, I write, to be perused best
 afterwards,
Tomb-leaves, body-leaves, growing up above me,
 above death,
Perennial roots, tall leaves—O the winter shall not freeze
 you, delicate leaves,
Every year shall you bloom again—Out from where you
 retired, you shall emerge again;
O I do not know whether many, passing by, will discover
 you, or inhale your faint odor—but I believe a few will;
O slender leaves! O blossoms of my blood! I permit you
 to tell, in your own way, of the heart that is under you,
O burning and throbbing—surely all will one day be
 accomplished;
O I do not know what you mean, there underneath
 yourselves—you are not happiness,
You are often more bitter than I can bear—you burn
 and sting me,
Yet you are very beautiful to me, you faint-tinged roots—
 you make me think of Death,
Death is beautiful from you—(what indeed is beautiful,
 except Death and Love?)
O I think it is not for life I am chanting here my chant
 of lovers—I think it must be for Death,
For how calm, how solemn it grows, to ascend to the
 atmosphere of lovers,
Death or life I am then indifferent—my Soul declines
 to prefer,
I am not sure but the high Soul of lovers welcomes death
 most;
Indeed, O Death, I think now these leaves mean precisely
 the same as you mean;

Line 8 was deleted in 1881

Grow up taller, sweet leaves, that I may see! Grow up
  out of my breast!
Spring away from the concealed heart there!
Do not fold yourselves so in your pink-tinged roots,
  timid leaves!
Do not remain down there so ashamed, herbage of my
  breast!
Come, I am determined to unbare this broad breast of
  mine—I have long enough stifled and choked;
Emblematic and capricious blades, I leave you—now you
  serve me not,
Away! I will say what I have to say, by itself,
I will escape from the sham that was proposed to me,
I will sound myself and comrades only—I will never again
  utter a call, only their call,
I will raise, with it, immortal reverberations through
  The States,
I will give an example to lovers, to take permanent shape
  and will through The States;
Through me shall the words be said to make death
  exhilarating,
Give me your tone therefore, O Death, that I may
  accord with it,
Give me yourself—for I see that you belong to me now
  above all, and are folded together above all—you Love
  and Death are,
Nor will I allow you to balk me any more with what
  I was calling life,
For now it is conveyed to me that you are the purports
  essential,
That you hide in these shifting forms of life, for reasons—
  and that they are mainly for you,
That you, beyond them, come forth, to remain, the real
  reality,
That behind the mask of materials you patiently wait,
  no matter how long,
That you will one day, perhaps, take control of all,
That you will perhaps dissipate this entire show of
  appearance,
That may be you are what it is all for—but it does not
  last so very long,
But you will last very long.

Long I Thought that Knowledge Alone Would Suffice

Long I thought that knowledge alone would suffice me—
  O if I could but obtain knowledge!
Then my lands engrossed me—Lands of the prairies,
  Ohio's land, the southern savannas, engrossed me—
  For them I would live—I would be their orator;
Then I met the examples of old and new heroes—I heard
  of warriors, sailors, and all dauntless persons—
  And it seemed to me that I too had it in me to be as
  dauntless as any—and would be so;
And then, to enclose all, it came to me to strike up the
  songs of the New World—And then I believed my
  life must be spent in singing;
But now take notice, land of the prairies, land of the
  south savannas, Ohio's land,
Take notice, you Kanuck woods—and you Lake Huron—
  and all that with you roll toward Niagara—and you
  Niagara also,
And you, Californian mountains—That you each and
  all find somebody else to be your singer of songs,
For I can be your singer of songs no longer—One who
  loves me is jealous of me, and withdraws me from
  all but love,
With the rest I dispense—I sever from what I thought
  would suffice me, for it does not—it is now empty
  and tasteless to me,
I heed knowledge, and the grandeur of The States,
  and the example of heroes, no more,
I am indifferent to my own songs—I will go with him
  I love,
It is to be enough for us that we are together—We never
  separate again.

This poem appeared only in the 1860 edition of *Leaves of Grass*

Hours Continuing Long, Sore and Heavy-Hearted

Hours continuing long, sore and heavy-hearted,
Hours of the dusk, when I withdraw to a lonesome and
  unfrequented spot, seating myself, leaning my face
  in my hands;
Hours sleepless, deep in the night, when I go forth,
  speeding swiftly the country roads, or through the city
  streets, or pacing miles and miles, stifling plaintive cries;
Hours discouraged, distracted—for the one I cannot
  content myself without, soon I saw him content
  himself without me;
Hours when I am forgotten, (O weeks and months are
  passing, but I believe I am never to forget!)
Sullen and suffering hours! (I am ashamed—but it is
  useless—I am what I am;)
Hours of my torment—I wonder if other men ever have
  the like, out of the like feelings?
Is there even one other like me—distracted—his friend,
  his lover, lost to him?
Is he too as I am now? Does he still rise in the morning,
  dejected, thinking who is lost to him? and at night,
  awaking, think who is lost?
Does he too harbor his friendship silent and endless?
  harbor his anguish and passion?   10
Does some stray reminder, or the casual mention of a
  name, bring the fit back upon him, taciturn and
  deprest?
Does he see himself reflected in me? In these hours,
  does he see the face of his hours reflected?

Like the preceding poem, this one was never reprinted after
1860. Undoubtedly the confessional nature of the chants was
an important reason for their omission in subsequent editions

Roots and Leaves
Themselves Alone

Calamus taste,
(For I must change the strain—these are not to be
    pensive leaves, but leaves of joy,)
Roots and leaves unlike any but themselves,
Scents brought to men and women from the wild woods,
    and from the pond-side,
Breast-sorrel and pinks of love—fingers that wind around
    tighter than vines,
Gushes from the throats of birds, hid in the foliage
    of trees, as the sun is risen,
Breezes of land and love—Breezes set from living shores
    out to you on the living sea—to you, O sailors!
Frost-mellowed berries, and Third Month twigs, offered
    fresh to young persons wandering out in the fields
    when the winter breaks up,
Love-buds, put before you and within you, whoever
    you are,
Buds to be unfolded on the old terms, 10
If you bring the warmth of the sun to them, they will
    open, and bring form, color, perfume, to you,
If you become the aliment and the wet, they will become
    flowers, fruits, tall branches and trees,
They are comprised in you just as much as in themselves—
    perhaps more than in themselves,
They are not comprised in one season or succession,
    but many successions,
They have come slowly up out of the earth and me,
    and are to come slowly up out of you.

Whitman removed the first two lines and the last three in
1867   8 **Third Month** March   12 **aliment** nourishment

Trickle Drops

O drops of me! trickle, slow drops,
Candid, from me falling—drip, bleeding drops,
From wounds made to free you whence you were prisoned,
From my face—from my forehead and lips,
From my breast—from within where I was concealed—
  Press forth, red drops—confession drops,
Stain every page—stain every song I sing, every word
  I say, bloody drops,
Let them know your scarlet heat—let them glisten,
Saturate them with yourself, all ashamed and wet,
Glow upon all I have written or shall write, bleeding
  drops,
Let it all be seen in your light, blushing drops.   10

I Saw in Louisiana a Live-Oak Growing

I saw in Louisiana a live-oak growing,
All alone stood it, and the moss hung down from the
  branches,
Without any companion it grew there, uttering joyous
  leaves of dark green,
And its look, rude, unbending, lusty, made me think
  of myself,
But I wondered how it could utter joyous leaves,
  standing alone there, without its friend, its lover near—
  for I knew I could not,

In 1867, the first line reads: "Trickle drops! my blue veins leaving!"

And I broke off a twig with a certain number of leaves
  upon it, and twined around it a little moss,
And brought it away—and I have placed it in sight
  in my room,
It is not needed to remind me as of my own dear friends,
(For I believe lately I think of little else than of them,)
Yet it remains to me a curious token—it makes me think
  of manly love;
For all that, and though the live-oak glistens there in
  Louisiana, solitary, in a wide flat space,
Uttering joyous leaves all its life, without a friend, a
  lover, near,
I know very well I could not.

We Two Boys Together Clinging

We two boys together clinging,
One the other never leaving,
Up and down the roads going—North and South
  excursions making,
Power enjoying—elbows stretching—fingers clutching,
Armed and fearless—eating, drinking, sleeping, loving,
No law less than ourselves owning—sailing, soldiering,
  thieving, threatening,
Misers, menials, priests alarming—air breathing, water
  drinking, on the turf or the sea-beach dancing,
With birds singing—With fishes swimming—With trees
  branching and leafing,
Cities wrenching, ease scorning, statutes mocking,
  feebleness chasing,
Fulfilling our foray.

Line 8 was omitted in 1867. In a manuscript version Whitman entitled the poem "Razzia," meaning "a plundering and destructive incursion," certainly a more accurate description of its contents than the present somewhat sentimental title

Earth, My Likeness

Earth! my likeness!
Though you look so impassive, ample and spheric there,
I now suspect that is not all;
I now suspect there is something fierce in you, eligible
    to burst forth;
For an athlete is enamoured of me—and I of him,
But toward him there is something fierce and terrible
    in me, eligible to burst forth,
I dare not tell it in words—not even in these songs.

Here the Frailest Leaves of Me

Here my last words, and the most baffling,
Here the frailest leaves of me, and yet my strongest-lasting,
Here I shade down and hide my thoughts—I do not
    expose them,
And yet they expose me more than all my other poems.

The first line was eliminated in 1867

Out of the Cradle Endlessly Rocking

Out of the cradle endlessly rocking,
Out of the mocking-bird's throat, the musical shuttle,
Out of the Ninth-month midnight,
Over the sterile sands and the fields beyond, where the child leaving his bed wander'd alone, bareheaded, barefoot,
Down from the shower'd halo,
Up from the mystic play of shadows twining and twisting as if they were alive,
Out from the patches of briers and blackberries,
From the memories of the bird that chanted to me,
From your memories sad brother, from the fitful risings and fallings I heard,
From under that yellow half-moon late-risen and swollen as if with tears, 10
From those beginning notes of yearning and love there in the mist,
From the thousand responses of my heart never to cease,
From the myriad thence-arous'd words,
From the word stronger and more delicious than any,
From such as now they start the scene revisiting,
As a flock, twittering, rising, or overhead passing,
Borne hither, ere all eludes me, hurriedly,
A man, yet by these tears a little boy again,
Throwing myself on the sand, confronting the waves,

First published as "A Child's Reminiscence" in the New York *Saturday Press* in 1859, and later called "A Word Out of the Sea" in 1860 and 1867. Originally the first line read: "Out of the rocked cradle." Line 182 was added in 1881 3 **Ninthmonth** September, but also a birth symbol

I, chanter of pains and joys, uniter of here and hereafter, 20
Taking all hints to use them, but swiftly leaping
  beyond them,
A reminiscence sing.

Once Paumanok,
When the lilac-scent was in the air and Fifth-month
  grass was growing,
Up this seashore in some briers,
Two feather'd guests from Alabama, two together,
And their nest, and four light-green eggs spotted with
  brown,
And every day the he-bird to and fro near at hand,
And every day the she-bird crouch'd on her nest,
  silent, with bright eyes,
And every day I, a curious boy, never too close, never
  disturbing them, 30
Cautiously peering, absorbing, translating.

Shine! shine! shine!
Pour down your warmth, great sun!
While we bask, we two together.

Two together!
Winds blow south, or winds blow north,
Day come white, or night come black,
Home, or rivers and mountains from home,
Singing all time, minding no time,
While we two keep together. 40

Till of a sudden,
May-be kill'd, unknown to her mate,
One forenoon the she-bird crouch'd not on the nest,
Nor return'd that afternoon, nor the next,
Nor ever appear'd again.

And thenceforward all summer in the sound of the sea,
And at night under the full of the moon in calmer
  weather,

---

23 **Paumanok** Indian name for Long Island

Out of the Cradle Endlessly Rocking

Over the hoarse surging of the sea,
Or flitting from brier to brier by day,
I saw, I heard at intervals the remaining one, the
    he-bird,
The solitary guest from Alabama.

Blow! blow! blow!
Blow up sea-winds along Paumanok's shore;
I wait and I wait till you blow my mate to me.

Yes, when the stars glisten'd,
All night long on the prong of a moss-scallop'd stake,
Down almost amid the slapping waves,
Sat the lone singer wonderful causing tears.

He call'd on his mate,
He pour'd forth the meanings which I of all men
    know.

Yes my brother I know,
The rest might not, but I have treasur'd every note,
For more than once dimly down to the beach gliding,
Silent, avoiding the moonbeams, blending myself with
    the shadows,
Recalling now the obscure shapes, the echoes, the
    sounds and sights after their sorts,
The white arms out in the breakers tirelessly tossing,
I, with bare feet, a child, the wind wafting my hair,
Listen'd long and long.

Listen'd to keep, to sing, now translating the notes,
Following you my brother.

Soothe! soothe! soothe!
Close on its wave soothes the wave behind,
And again another behind embracing and lapping,
    every one close,
But my love soothes not me, not me.

Low hangs the moon, it rose late,
It is lagging—O I think it is heavy with love, with love.

O madly the sea pushes upon the land,
With love, with love.

O night! do I not see my love fluttering out among the breakers?
What is that little black thing I see there in the white?

Loud! loud! loud!
Loud I call to you, my love!

High and clear I shoot my voice over the waves,
Surely you must know who is here, is here,
You must know who I am, my love.
Low-hanging moon!
What is that dusky spot in your brown yellow?
O it is the shape, the shape of my mate!
O moon do not keep her from me any longer.

Land! land! O land!
Whichever way I turn, O I think you could give me my mate back again if you only would,
For I am almost sure I see her dimly whichever way I look.

O rising stars!
Perhaps the one I want so much will rise, will rise with some of you.

O throat! O trembling throat!
Sound clearer through the atmosphere!
Pierce the woods, the earth,
Somewhere listening to catch you must be the one I want.

Shake out carols!
Solitary here, the night's carols!
Carols of lonesome love! death's carols!
Carols under that lagging, yellow, waning moon!
O under that moon where she droops almost down into the sea!
O reckless despairing carols.

Out of the Cradle Endlessly Rocking

But soft! sink low!
Soft! let me just murmur,
And do you wait a moment you husky-nois'd sea,
For somewhere I believe I heard my mate responding to me,
So faint, I must be still, be still to listen,
But not altogether still, for then she might not come immediately to me.

Hither my love!
Here I am! here!
With this just-sustain'd note I announce myself to you,
This gentle call is for you my love, for you.

Do not be decoy'd elsewhere,
That is the whistle of the wind, it is not my voice,
That is the fluttering, the fluttering of the spray,
Those are the shadows of leaves.

O darkness! O in vain!
O I am very sick and sorrowful.

O brown halo in the sky near the moon, drooping upon the sea!
O troubled reflection in the sea!
O throat! O throbbing heart!
And I singing uselessly, uselessly all the night.

O past! O happy life! O songs of joy!
In the air, in the woods, over fields,
Loved! loved! loved! loved! loved!
But my mate no more, no more with me!
We two together no more.

The aria sinking,
All else continuing, the stars shining,
The winds blowing, the notes of the bird continuous echoing,
With angry moans the fierce old mother incessantly moaning,
On the sands of Paumanok's shore gray and rustling,

The yellow half-moon enlarged, sagging down, drooping,
    the face of the sea almost touching,
The boy ecstatic, with his bare feet the waves, with his
    hair the atmosphere dallying,
The love in the heart long pent, now loose, now at last
    tumultuously bursting,
The aria's meaning, the ears, the soul, swiftly
    depositing,
The strange tears down the cheeks coursing,
The colloquy there, the trio, each uttering,
The undertone, the savage old mother incessantly crying,
To the boy's soul's questions sullenly timing, some
    drown'd secret hissing,
To the outsetting bard.

Demon or bird! (said the boy's soul,)
Is it indeed toward your mate you sing? or is it really
    to me?
For I, that was a child, my tongue's use sleeping,
    now I have heard you,
Now in a moment I know what I am for, I awake,
And already a thousand singers, a thousand songs,
    clearer, louder and more sorrowful than yours,
A thousand warbling echoes have started to life
    within me, never to die.

O you singer solitary, singing by yourself, projecting me,
O solitary me listening, never more shall I cease
    perpetuating you,
Never more shall I escape, never more the reverberations,
Never more the cries of unsatisfied love be absent
    from me,
Never again leave me to be the peaceful child I was
    before what there in the night,
By the sea under the yellow and sagging moon,
The messenger there arous'd, the fire, the sweet hell
    within,
The unknown want, the destiny of me.

O give me the clew! (it lurks in the night here
    somewhere,)
O if I am to have so much, let me have more!

A word then, (for I will conquer it,) 160
The word final, superior to all,
Subtle, sent up—what is it?—I listen;
Are you whispering it, and have been all the time, you
    sea-waves?
Is that it from your liquid rims and wet sands?

Whereto answering, the sea,
Delaying not, hurrying not,
Whisper'd me through the night, and very plainly
    before daybreak,
Lisp'd to me the low and delicious word death,
And again death, death, death, death,
Hissing melodious, neither like the bird nor like my
    arous'd child's heart, 170
But edging near as privately for me rustling at my feet,
Creeping thence steadily up to my ears and laving me
    softly all over,
Death, death, death, death, death.

Which I do not forget,
But fuse the song of my dusky demon and brother,
That he sang to me in the moonlight on Paumanok's
    gray beach,
With the thousand responsive songs at random,
My own songs awaked from that hour,
And with them the key, the word up from the waves,
The word of the sweetest song and all songs, 180
That strong and delicious word which, creeping to my
    feet,
(Or like some old crone rocking the cradle, swathed in
    sweet garments, bending aside,)
The sea whisper'd me.

from Drum-Taps

Vigil Strange I Kept on the Field One Night

Vigil strange I kept on the field one night,
When you, my son and my comrade, dropt at my side that day,
One look I but gave, which your dear eyes return'd, with a look I shall never forget;
One touch of your hand to mine, O boy, reach'd up as you lay on the ground;
Then onward I sped in the battle, the even-contested battle;
Till late in the night reliev'd, to the place at last again I made my way;
Found you in death so cold, dear comrade—found your body, son of responding kisses, (never again on earth responding:)
Bared your face in the starlight—curious the scene—cool blew the moderate night-wind;
Long there and then in vigil I stood, dimly around me the battle-field spreading;
Vigil wondrous and vigil sweet, there in the fragrant silent night;   10
But not a tear fell, not even a long-drawn sigh—Long, long I gazed;
Then on the earth partially reclining, sat by your side, leaning my chin in my hands;
Passing sweet hours, immortal and mystic hours with you, dearest comrade—Not a tear, not a word;
Vigil of silence, love and death—vigil for you, my son and my soldier,

As onward silently stars aloft, eastward new ones
    upward stole;
Vigil final for you, brave boy, (I could not save you,
    swift was your death,
I faithfully loved you and cared for you living—I
    think we shall surely meet again;)
Till at latest lingering of the night, indeed just as the
    dawn appear'd,
My comrade I wrapt in his blanket, envelop'd well his
    form,
Folded the blanket well, tucking it carefully over head,
    and carefully under feet;   20
And there and then, and bathed by the rising sun, my
    son in his grave, in his rude-dug grave I deposited;
Ending my vigil strange with that—vigil of night and
    battle-field dim;
Vigil for boy of responding kisses, (never again on earth
    responding;)
Vigil for comrade swiftly slain—vigil I never forget,
    how as day brighten'd,
I rose from the chill ground, and folded my soldier well
    in his blanket,
And buried him where he fell.

Over the Carnage Rose Prophetic a Voice

1 Over the carnage rose prophetic a voice,
    Be not dishearten'd—Affection shall solve the problems
        of Freedom yet;
    Those who love each other shall become invincible—
        they shall yet make Columbia victorious.

This poem is basically a rearrangement of a "Calamus" poem
(1860); see *Leaves of Grass—Comprehensive Reader's Edition*

2 Sons of the Mother of All! you shall yet be victorious!
You shall yet laugh to scorn the attacks of all the
   remainder of the earth.

3 No danger shall balk Columbia's lovers;
If need be, a thousand shall sternly immolate themselves
   for one.

4 One from Massachusetts shall be a Missourian's
   comrade;
From Maine and from hot Carolina, and another an
   Oregonese, shall be friends triune,
More precious to each other than all the riches of the
   earth.

5 To Michigan, Florida perfumes shall tenderly come;
Not the perfumes of flowers, but sweeter, and wafted
   beyond death.

6 It shall be customary in the houses and streets to see
   manly affection;
The most dauntless and rude shall touch face to face
   lightly;
The dependence of Liberty shall be lovers,
The continuance of Equality shall be comrades.

7 These shall tie you and band you stronger than hoops
   of iron;
I, extatic, O partners! O lands! with the love of
   lovers tie you.

8 Were you looking to be held together by the lawyers?
Or by an agreement on a paper? or by arms?
—Nay—nor the world, nor any living thing, will so
   cohere.

By the Bivouac's Fitful Flame

By the bivouac's fitful flame,
A procession winding around me, solemn and sweet
    and slow;—but first I note,
The tents of the sleeping army, the fields' and woods'
    dim outline,
The darkness, lit by spots of kindled fire—the silence;
Like a phantom far or near an occasional figure moving;
The shrubs and trees, (as I left my eyes they seem to be
    stealthily watching me;)
While wind in procession thoughts, O tender and
    wond'rous thoughts,
Of life and death—of home and the past and loved,
    and of those that are far away;
A solemn and slow procession there as I sit on the
    ground,
By the bivouac's fitful flame.

As I Lay with My Head in Your Lap Camerado

As I lay with my head in your lap, camerado,
The confession I made I resume—what I said to you and
    the open air I resume:
I know I am restless, and make others so;
I know my words are weapons, full of danger, full of
    death;
(Indeed I am myself the real soldier;
It is not he, there, with his bayonet, and not the
    red-striped artilleryman;)

For I confront peace, security, and all the settled laws, to
    unsettle them;
I am more resolute because all have denied me, than
    I could ever have been had all accepted me;
I heed not, and have never heeded, either experience,
    cautions, majorities, nor ridicule;
And the threat of what is call'd hell is little or nothing
    to me;
And the lure of what is call'd heaven is little or nothing
    to me;
. . . Dear camerado! I confess I have urged you onward
    with me, and still urge you, without the least idea
    what is our destination,
Or whether we shall be victorious, or utterly quell'd and
    defeated.

Dirge for Two Veterans

1   The last sunbeam
    Lightly falls from the finish'd Sabbath,
    On the pavement here—and there beyond, it is looking,
    Down a new-made double grave.

2   Lo! the moon ascending!
    Up from the east, the silvery round moon;
    Beautiful over the house-tops, ghastly, phantom moon;
    Immense and silent moon.

3   I see a sad procession,
    And I hear the sound of coming full-key'd bugles;
    All the channels of the city streets they're flooding,
    As with voices and with tears.

One of the first poems of Whitman to be set to music, by
Frédéric Louis Ritter (1834–91), professor of music at Vassar

4 I hear the great drums pounding,
　And the small drums steady whirring;
　And every blow of the great convulsive drums,
　Strikes me through and through.

5 For the son is brought with the father;
　(In the foremost ranks of the fierce assault they fell;
　Two veterans, son and father, dropt together,
　And the double grave awaits them.)

6 Now nearer blow the bugles,
　And the drums strike more convulsive;
　And the day-light o'er the pavement quite has faded,
　And the strong dead-march enwraps me.

7 In the eastern sky up-buoying,
　The sorrowful vast phantom moves illumin'd;
　('Tis some mother's large, transparent face,
　In heaven brighter growing.)

8 O strong dead-march, you please me!
　O moon immense, with your silvery face you soothe me!
　O my soldiers twain! O my veterans, passing to burial!
　What I have I also give you.

9 The moon gives you light,
　And the bugles and the drums give you music;
　And my heart, O my soldiers, my veterans,
　My heart gives you love.

When Lilacs Last in the Dooryard Bloom'd

1 When lilacs last in the dooryard bloom'd,
  And the great star early droop'd in the western sky in the night,
  I mourn'd, and yet shall mourn with ever-returning spring.

Ever-returning spring, trinity sure to me you bring,
Lilac blooming perennial and drooping star in the west,
And thought of him I love.

2 O powerful western fallen star!
  O shades of night—O moody, tearful night!
  O great star disappear'd—O the black murk that hides the star!
  O cruel hands that hold me powerless—O helpless soul of me!
  O harsh surrounding cloud that will not free my soul.

3 In the dooryard fronting an old farm-house near the white-wash'd palings,
  Stands the lilac-bush tall-growing with heart-shaped leaves of rich green,
  With many a pointed blossom rising delicate, with the perfume strong I love,
  With every leaf a miracle—and from this bush in the dooryard,

4 **trinity** the three basic symbols of the poem, lilac, star (Venus), and the bird (thrush)

With delicate-color'd blossoms and heart-shaped leaves of
    rich green,
A sprig with its flower I break.

4   In the swamp in secluded recesses,
    A shy and hidden bird is warbling a song.

    Solitary the thrush,
    The hermit withdrawn to himself, avoiding the
        settlements,
    Sings by himself a song.

    Song of the bleeding throat,
    Death's outlet song of life, (for well dear brother I know,
    If thou wast not granted to sing thou would'st surely
        die.)

5   Over the breast of the spring, the land, amid cities,
    Amid lanes and through old woods, where lately the
        violets peep'd from the ground, spotting the gray
        debris,
    Amid the grass in the fields each side of the lanes,
        passing the endless grass,
    Passing the yellow-spear'd wheat, every grain from its
        shroud in the dark-brown fields uprisen,
    Passing the apple-tree blows of white and pink in the
        orchards,
    Carrying a corpse to where it shall rest in the grave,
    Night and day journeys a coffin.

6   Coffin that passes through lanes and streets,
    Through day and night with the great cloud darkening
        the land,
    With the pomp of the inloop'd flags with the cities
        draped in black,

26–45 Lincoln's coffin was carried by railroad from Washington
to Springfield, Illinois

With the show of the States themselves as of crape-veil'd
  women standing,
With processions long and winding and the flambeaus
  of the night,
With the countless torches lit, with the silent sea of
  faces and the unbared heads,
With the waiting depot, the arriving coffin, and the
  sombre faces,
With dirges through the night, with the thousand voices
  rising strong and solemn, 40
With all the mournful voices of the dirges pour'd
  around the coffin,
The dim-lit churches and the shuddering organs—where
  amid these you journey,
With the tolling tolling bells' perpetual clang,
Here, coffin that slowly passes,
I give you my sprig of lilac.

7 (Nor for you, for one alone,
Blossoms and branches green to coffins all I bring,
For fresh as the morning, thus would I chant a song for
  you O sane and sacred death.

All over bouquets of roses,
O death, I cover you over with roses and early lilies, 50
But mostly and now the lilac that blooms the first,
Copious I break, I break the sprigs from the bushes,
With loaded arms I come, pouring for you,
For you and the coffins all of you O death.)

8 O western orb sailing the heaven,
  Now I know what you must have meant as a month
    since I walk'd,
  As I walk'd in silence the transparent shadowy night,
  As I saw you had something to tell as you bent to me
    night after night,
  As you droop'd from the sky low down as if to my side,
    (while the other stars all look'd on,)
  As we wander'd together the solemn night, (for
    something I know not what kept me from sleep,) 60

When Lilacs Last in the Dooryard Bloom'd

As the night advanced, and I saw on the rim of the
   west how full you were of woe,
As I stood on the rising ground in the breeze in the
   cool transparent night,
As I watch'd where you pass'd and was lost in the
   netherward black of the night,
As my soul in its trouble dissatisfied sank, as where you
   sad orb,
Concluded, dropt in the night, and was gone.

9 Sing on there in the swamp,
   O singer bashful and tender, I hear your notes, I hear
      your call,
   I hear, I come presently, I understand you,
   But a moment I linger, for the lustrous star has detain'd
      me,
   The star my departing comrade holds and detains me.   70

10 O how shall I warble myself for the dead one there I
       loved?
    And how shall I deck my song for the large sweet soul
       that has gone?
    And what shall my perfume be for the grave of him I
       love?

    Sea-winds blown from east and west,
    Blown from the Eastern sea and blown from the
       Western sea, till there on the prairies meeting,
    These and with these and the breath of my chant,
    I'll perfume the grave of him I love.

11 O what shall I hang on the chamber walls?
    And what shall the pictures be that I hang on the walls,
    To adorn the burial-house of him I love?   80

   80 **burial-house** the tombs of pharaohs were adorned with pictures symbolic of life and death

Pictures of growing spring and farms and homes,
With the Fourth-month eve at sundown, and the gray
  smoke lucid and bright,
With floods of the yellow gold of the gorgeous, indolent,
  sinking sun, burning, expanding the air,
With the fresh sweet herbage under foot, and the pale
  green leaves of the trees prolific,
In the distance the flowing glaze, the breast of the river,
  with a wind-dapple here and there,
With ranging hills on the banks, with many a line
  against the sky, and shadows,
And the city at hand with dwellings so dense, and
  stacks of chimneys,
And all the scenes of life and the workshops, and the
  workmen homeward returning.

12 Lo, body and soul—this land,
  My own Manhattan with spires, and the sparkling and
    hurrying tides, and the ships,
  The varied and ample land, the South and the North in
    the light, Ohio's shores and flashing Missouri,
  And ever the far-spreading prairies cover'd with grass
    and corn.

  Lo, the most excellent sun so calm and haughty,
  The violet and purple morn with just-felt breezes,
  The gentle soft-born measureless light,
  The miracle spreading bathing all, the fulfill'd noon,
  The coming eve delicious, the welcome night and the
    stars,
  Over my cities shining all, enveloping man and land.

13 Sing on, sing on you gray-brown bird,
  Sing from the swamps, the recesses, pour your chant
    from the bushes,
  Limitless out of the dusk, out of the cedars and pines.

When Lilacs Last in the Dooryard Bloom'd

Sing on dearest brother, warble your reedy song,
Loud human song, with voice of uttermost woe.

O liquid and free and tender!
O wild and loose to my soul—O wondrous singer!
You only I hear—yet the star holds me, (but will soon depart,)
Yet the lilac with mastering odor holds me.

14 Now while I sat in the day and look'd forth,
In the close of the day with its light and the fields of spring, and the farmers preparing their crops,
In the large unconscious scenery of my land with its lakes and forests,
In the heavenly aerial beauty, (after the perturb'd winds and the storms,)
Under the arching heavens of the afternoon swift passing, and the voices of children and women,
The many-moving sea-tides, and I saw the ships how they sail'd,
And the summer approaching with richness, and the fields all busy with labor,
And the infinite separate houses, how they all went on, each with its meals and minutia of daily usages,
And the streets how their throbbings throbb'd, and the cities pent—lo, then and there,
Falling upon them all and among them all, enveloping me with the rest,
Appear'd the cloud, appear'd the long black trail,
And I knew death, its thought, and the sacred knowledge of death.

Then with the knowledge of death as walking one side of me,
And the thought of death close-walking the other side of me,
And I in the middle as with companions, and as holding the hands of companions,
I fled forth to the hiding receiving night that talks not,

Down to the shores of the water, the path by the swamp
  in the dimness,
To the solemn shadowy cedars and ghostly pines so
  still.

And the singer so shy to the rest receiv'd me,
The gray-brown bird I know receiv'd us comrades three,
And he sang the carol of death, and a verse for him I
  love.

From deep secluded recesses,
From the fragrant cedars and the ghostly pines so still,   130
Came the carol of the bird.

And the charm of the carol rapt me,
As I held as if by their hands my comrades in the night,
And the voice of my spirit tallied the song of the bird.

Come lovely and soothing death,
Undulate round the world, serenely arriving, arriving,
In the day, in the night, to all, to each,
Sooner or later delicate death.

Prais'd be the fathomless universe,
For life and joy, and for objects and knowledge curious,   140
And for love, sweet love—but praise! praise! praise!
For the sure-enwinding arms of cool-enfolding death.

Dark mother always gliding near with soft feet,
Have none chanted for thee a chant of fullest welcome?
Then I chant it for thee, I glorify thee above all,
I bring thee a song that when thou must indeed come,
  come unfalteringly.

Approach strong deliveress,
When it is so, when thou hast taken them I joyously
  sing the dead,
Lost in the loving floating ocean of thee,
Laved in the flood of thy bliss O death.   150

When Lilacs Last in the Dooryard Bloom'd   135

From me to thee glad serenades,
Dances for thee I propose saluting thee, adornments
   and feastings for thee,
And the sights of the open landscape and the high-spread
   sky are fitting,
And life and the fields, and the huge and thoughtful
   night.

The night in silence under many a star,
The ocean shore and the husky whispering wave whose
   voice I know,
And the soul turning to thee O vast and well-veil'd
   death,
And the body gratefully nestling close to thee.

Over the tree-tops I float thee a song,
Over the rising and sinking waves, over the myriad
   fields and the prairies wide,   160
Over the dense-pack'd cities all and the teeming wharves
   and ways,
I float this carol with joy, with joy to thee O death.

15 To the tally of my soul,
    Loud and strong kept up the gray-brown bird,
    With pure deliberate notes spreading filling the night.

    Loud in the pines and cedars dim,
    Clear in the freshness moist and the swamp-perfume,
    And I with my comrades there in the night.

    While my sight that was bound in my eyes unclosed,
    As to long panoramas of visions.   170

    And I saw askant the armies,
    I saw as in noiseless dreams hundreds of battle-flags,
    Borne through the smoke of the battle and pierc'd
       with missiles I saw them,
    And carried hither and yon through the smoke, and
       torn and bloody,

---

171 **askant** obliquely, or perhaps distrustfully

And at last but a few shreds left on the staffs, (and all
    in silence,)
And the staffs all splinter'd and broken.

I saw battle-corpses, myriads of them,
And the white skeletons of young men, I saw them,
I saw the debris and debris of all the slain soldiers of
    the war,
But I saw they were not as was thought,   180
They themselves were fully at rest, they suffer'd not,
The living remain'd and suffer'd, the mother suffer'd,
And the wife and the child and the musing comrade
    suffer'd,
And the armies that remain'd suffer'd.

16 Passing the visions, passing the night,
    Passing, unloosing the hold of my comrades' hands,
    Passing the song of the hermit bird and the tallying
        song of my soul,
    Victorious song, death's outlet song, yet varying
        ever-altering song,
    As low and wailing, yet clear the notes, rising and
        falling, flooding the night,
    Sadly sinking and fainting, as warning and warning,
        and yet again bursting with joy,   190
    Covering the earth and filling the spread of the heaven,
    As that powerful psalm in the night I heard from
        recesses,
    Passing, I leave thee lilac with heart-shaped leaves,
    I leave thee there in the door-yard, blooming, returning
        with spring.

I cease from my song for thee,
From my gaze on thee in the west, fronting the west,
    communing with thee,
O comrade lustrous with silver face in the night.

Yet each to keep and all, retrievements out of the night,
The song, the wondrous chant of the gray-brown bird,

And the tallying chant, the echo arous'd in my soul,   200
With the lustrous and drooping star with the countenance full of woe,
With the holders holding my hand nearing the call of the bird,
Comrades mine and I in the midst, and their memory ever to keep, for the dead I loved so well,
For the sweetest, wisest soul of all my days and lands —and this for his dear sake,
Lilac and star and bird twined with the chant of my soul,
There in the fragrant pines and the cedars dusk and dim.

Passage to India

1 Singing my days,
Singing the great achievements of the present,
Singing the strong light works of engineers,
Our modern wonders, (the antique ponderous Seven outvied,)
In the Old World the east the Suez canal,
The New by its mighty railroad spann'd,
The seas inlaid with eloquent gentle wires;
Yet first to sound, and ever sound, the cry with thee O soul,
The Past! the Past! the Past!

The Past—the dark unfathom'd retrospect! 10
The teeming gulf—the sleepers and the shadows!
The past—the infinite greatness of the past!
For what is the present after all but a growth out of the past?
(As a projectile form'd, impell'd, passing a certain line, still keeps on,
So the present, utterly form'd, impell'd by the past.)

First published in 1871, although parts were composed as early as 1868. To his friend Horace Traubel, Whitman observed: "There's more of me, the essential ultimate me, in that than in any of the poems. There is no philosophy, consistent or inconsistent, in that poem . . . but the burden of it is evolution—the one thing escaping the other—the unfolding of cosmic purposes" 5 **Suez** the canal was opened on November 17, 1869 6 **railroad** the Union Pacific and Central Pacific railroads were linked on May 10, 1869 7 **wires** the Atlantic cable was laid in 1866

2   Passage O soul to India!
Eclaircise the myths Asiatic, the primitive fables.

Not you alone proud truths of the world,
Nor you alone ye facts of modern science,
But myths and fables of eld, Asia's, Africa's fables, 20
The far-darting beams of the spirit, the unloos'd dreams,
The deep diving bibles and legends,
The daring plots of the poets, the elder religions;
O you temples fairer than lilies pour'd over by the
    rising sun!
O you fables spurning the known, eluding the hold of
    the known, mounting to heaven!
You lofty and dazzling towers, pinnacled, red as roses,
    burnish'd with gold!
Towers of fables immortal fashion'd from mortal dreams!
You too I welcome and fully the same as the rest!
You too with joy I sing.

Passage to India! 30
Lo, soul, seest thou not God's purpose from the first?
The earth to be spann'd, connected by network,
The races, neighbors, to marry and be given in marriage,
The oceans to be cross'd, the distant brought near,
The lands to be welded together.

A worship new I sing,
You captains, voyagers, explorers, yours,
You engineers, you architects, machinists, yours,
You, not for trade or transportation only,
But in God's name, and for thy sake O soul. 40

3   Passage to India!
Lo soul for thee of tableaus twain,
I see in one the Suez canal initiated, open'd,
I see the procession of steamships, the Empress
    Eugenie's leading the van,
I mark from on deck the strange landscape, the pure
    sky, the level sand in the distance,

17 **Eclaircise** clarify (French)

I pass swiftly the picturesque groups, the workmen gather'd,
The gigantic dredging machines.

In one again, different, (yet thine, all thine, O soul, the same,)
I see over my own continent the Pacific railroad surmounting every barrier,
I see continual trains of cars winding along the Platte carrying freight and passengers,   50
I hear the locomotives rushing and roaring, and the shrill steam-whistle,
I hear the echoes reverberate through the grandest scenery in the world,
I cross the Laramie plains, I note the rocks in grotesque shapes, the buttes,
I see the plentiful larkspur and wild onions, the barren, colorless, sage-deserts,
I see in glimpses afar or towering immediately above me the great mountains, I see the Wind river and the Wahsatch mountains,
I see the Monument mountain and the Eagle's Nest, I pass the Promontory, I ascend the Nevadas,
I scan the noble Elk mountain and wind around its base,
I see the Humboldt range, I thread the valley and cross the river,
I see the clear waters of lake Tahoe, I see forests of majestic pines,
Or crossing the great desert, the alkaline plains, I behold enchanting mirages of waters and meadows,   60
Marking through these and after all, in duplicate slender lines,
Bridging the three or four thousand miles of land travel,
Tying the Eastern to the Western sea,
The road between Europe and Asia.

49 **barrier** this and the following lines describe the route of the new railroad from Omaha to the West Coast

(Ah Genoese thy dream! thy dream!
Centuries after thou art laid in thy grave,
The shore thou foundest verifies thy dream.)

4 Passage to India!
Struggles of many a captain, tales of many a sailor dead,
Over my mood stealing and spreading they come, 70
Like clouds and cloudlets in the unreach'd sky.

Along all history, down the slopes,
As a rivulet running, sinking now, and now again to
   the surface rising,
A ceaseless thought, a varied train—lo, soul, to thee,
   thy sight, they rise,
The plans, the voyages again, the expeditions;
Again Vasco de Gama sails forth,
Again the knowledge gain'd, the mariner's compass,
Lands found and nations born, thou born America,
For purpose vast, man's long probation fill'd,
Thou rondure of the world at last accomplish'd. 80

5 O vast Rondure, swimming in space,
Cover'd all over with visible power and beauty,
Alternate light and day and the teeming spiritual
   darkness,
Unspeakable high processions of sun and moon and
   countless stars above,
Below, the manifold grass and waters, animals, mountains,
   trees,
With inscrutable purpose, some hidden prophetic
   intention,
Now first it seems my thought begins to span thee.
Down from the gardens of Asia descending radiating,
Adam and Eve appear, then their myriad progeny after
   them,

---

65 **Genoese** Christopher Columbus 76 **Vasco de Gama** da
Gama (1469?–1524), Portuguese navigator, who made the first
voyage from Europe to India around the Cape of Good Hope

Wandering, yearning, curious, with restless explorations,
With questionings, baffled, formless, feverish, with
  never-happy hearts,
With that sad incessant refrain, *Wherefore unsatisfied
  soul?* and *Whither O mocking life?*

Ah who shall soothe these feverish children?
Who justify these restless explorations?
Who speak the secret of impassive earth?
Who bind it to us? what is this separate Nature so
  unnatural?
What is this earth to our affections? (unloving earth,
  without a throb to answer ours,
Cold earth, the place of graves.)

Yet soul be sure the first intent remains, and shall be
  carried out,
Perhaps even now the time has arrived.

After the seas are all cross'd, (as they seem already
  cross'd,)
After the great captains and engineers have accomplish'd
  their work,
After the noble inventors, after the scientists, the
  chemist, the geologist, ethnologist,
Finally shall come the poet worthy that name,
The true son of God shall come singing his songs.

Then not your deeds only O voyagers, O scientists and
  inventors, shall be justified,
All these hearts as of fretted children shall be sooth'd,
All affection shall be fully responded to, the secret shall
  be told,
All these separations and gaps shall be taken up and
  hook'd and link'd together,
The whole earth, this cold, impassive, voiceless earth,
  shall be completely justified,
Trinitas divine shall be gloriously accomplish'd and
  compacted by the true son of God, the poet,
(He shall indeed pass the straits and conquer the
  mountains,

Passage to India 143

He shall double the cape of Good Hope to some purpose,)
Nature and Man shall be disjoin'd and diffused no
  more,
The true son of God shall absolutely fuse them.

6 Year at whose wide-flung door I sing!
Year of the purpose accomplish'd!
Year of the marriage of continents, climates and oceans!
(No mere doge of Venice now wedding the Adriatic,)
I see O year in you the vast terraqueous globe given
  and giving all,
Europe to Asia, Africa join'd, and they to the New
  World,
The lands, geographies, dancing before you, holding a
  festival garland,
As brides and bridegrooms hand in hand.

Passage to India!
Cooling airs from Caucasus far, soothing cradle of man,
The river Euphrates flowing, the past lit up again.

Lo soul, the retrospect brought forward,
The old, most populous, wealthiest of earth's lands,
The streams of the Indus and the Ganges and their
  many affluents,
(I my shores of America walking to-day behold, resuming
  all,)
The tale of Alexander on his warlike marches suddenly
  dying,
On one side China and on the other side Persia and
  Arabia,
To the south the great seas and the bay of Bengal,
The flowing literatures, tremendous epics, religions,
  castes,
Old occult Brahma interminably far back, the tender
  and junior Buddha,

126 **Euphrates** cradle of Western civilization 131 **Alexander**
Alexander the Great (356–323 B.C.) died shortly after his
invasion of India

Central and southern empires and all their belongings, possessors,
The wars of Tamerlane, the reign of Aurungzebe,
The traders, rulers, explorers, Moslems, Venetians, Byzantium, the Arabs, Portuguese,
The first travelers famous yet, Marco Polo, Batouta the Moor,
Doubts to be solv'd, the map incognita, blanks to be fill'd, 140
The foot of man unstay'd, the hands never at rest,
Thyself O soul that will not brook a challenge.

The mediæval navigators rise before me,
The world of 1492, with its awaken'd enterprise,
Something swelling in humanity now like the sap of the earth in spring,
The sunset splendor of chivalry declining.

And who art thou sad shade?
Gigantic, visionary, thyself a visionary,
With majestic limbs and pious beaming eyes,
Spreading around with every look of thine a golden world, 150
Enhuing it with gorgeous hues.

As the chief histrion,
Down to the footlights walk in some great scena,
Dominating the rest I see the Admiral himself,
(History's type of courage, action, faith,)
Behold him sail from Palos leading his little fleet,
His voyage behold, his return, his great fame,
His misfortunes, calumniators, behold him a prisoner, chain'd,
Behold his dejection, poverty, death.

---

137 **Tamerlane** "Timur the Lame" (1336?–1405) led his armies to India in 1398 **Aurungzebe** "Conqueror of the World" (1618–1707) 139 **Marco Polo** Italian traveler (1254?–1324) who journeyed throughout Asia **Batouta** Ibn Batuta, greatest of Moslem travelers (1304–78) 147 **sad shade** Columbus 152 **histrion** actor 156 **Palos** Spanish port from which Columbus sailed in 1492

(Curious in time I stand, noting the efforts of heroes,   160
Is the deferment long? bitter the slander, poverty, death?
Lies the seed unreck'd for centuries in the ground? lo,
   to God's due occasion,
Uprising in the night, it sprouts, blooms,
And fills the earth with use and beauty.)

7 Passage indeed O soul to primal thought,
Not lands and seas alone, thy own clear freshness,
The young maturity of brood and bloom,
To realms of budding bibles.

O soul, repressless, I with thee and thou with me,
Thy circumnavigation of the world begin,   170
Of man, the voyage of his mind's return,
To reason's early paradise,
Back, back to wisdom's birth, to innocent intuitions,
Again with fair creation.

8 O we can wait no longer,
We too take ship O soul,
Joyous we too launch out on trackless seas,
Fearless for unknown shores on waves of ecstasy to sail,
Amid the wafting winds, (thou pressing me to thee, I
   thee to me, O soul,)
Caroling free, singing our song of God,   180
Chanting our chant of pleasant exploration.

With laugh and many a kiss,
(Let others deprecate, let others weep for sin, remorse,
   humiliation,)
O soul thou pleasest me, I thee.

Ah more than any priest O soul we too believe in God,
But with the mystery of God we dare not dally.

O soul thou pleasest me, I thee,
Sailing these seas or on the hills, or waking in the night,

Thoughts, silent thoughts, of Time and Space and Death,
   like waters flowing,
Bear me indeed as through the regions infinite, 190
Whose air I breathe, whose ripples hear, lave me all
   over,
Bathe me O God in thee, mounting to thee,
I and my soul to range in range of thee.

O Thou transcendent,
Nameless, the fibre and the breath,
Light of the light, shedding forth universes, thou
   centre of them,
Thou mightier centre of the true, the good, the loving,
Thou moral, spiritual fountain—affection's source—thou
   reservoir,
(O pensive soul of me—O thirst unsatisfied—waitest
   not there?
Waitest not haply for us somewhere there the Comrade
   perfect?) 200
Thou pulse—thou motive of the stars, suns, systems,
That, circling, move in order, safe, harmonious,
Athwart the shapeless vastnesses of space,
How should I think, how breathe a single breath, how
   speak, if, out of myself,
I could not launch, to those, superior universes?

Swiftly I shrivel at the thought of God,
At Nature and its wonders, Time and Space and Death,
But that I, turning, call to thee O soul, thou actual
   Me,
And lo, thou gently masterest the orbs,
Thou matest Time, smilest content at Death, 210
And fillest, swellest full the vastnesses of Space.

Greater than stars or suns,
Bounding O soul thou journeyest forth;
What love than thine and ours could wider amplify?
What aspirations, wishes, outvie thine and ours O soul?
What dreams of the ideal? what plans of purity,
   perfection, strength?
What cheerful willingness for others' sake to give up all?
For others' sake to suffer all?

Reckoning ahead O soul, when thou, the time achiev'd,
The seas all cross'd, weather'd the capes, the voyage
   done,
Surrounded, copest, frontest God, yieldest, the aim
   attain'd,
As fill'd with friendship, love complete, the Elder
   Brother found,
The Younger melts in fondness in his arms.

9 Passage to more than India!
Are thy wings plumed indeed for such far flights?
O soul, voyagest thou indeed on voyages like those?
Disportest thou on waters such as those?
Soundest below the Sanscrit and the Vedas?
Then have thy bent unleash'd.

Passage to you, your shores, ye aged fierce enigmas!
Passage to you, to mastership of you, ye strangling
   problems!
You, strew'd with the wrecks of skeletons, that, living,
   never reach'd you.

Passage to more than India!
O secret of the earth and sky!
Of you O waters of the sea! O winding creeks and rivers!
Of you O woods and fields! of you strong mountains of
   my land!
Of you O prairies! of you gray rocks!
O morning red! O clouds! O rain and snows!
O day and night, passage to you!

O sun and moon and all you stars! Sirius and Jupiter!
Passage to you!

Passage, immediate passage! the blood burns in my veins!
Away O soul! hoist instantly the anchor!
Cut the hawsers—haul out—shake out every sail!

---

228 **Sanscrit . . . Vedas** ancient sacred writings of the Hindus
in Sanskrit   229 **bent** disposition or inclination

Have we not stood here like trees in the ground long
    enough?
Have we not grovel'd here long enough, eating and
    drinking like mere brutes?
Have we not darken'd and dazed ourselves with books
    long enough?

Sail forth—steer for the deep waters only,
Reckless O soul, exploring, I with thee, and thou with me,
For we are bound where mariner has not yet dared to go, 250
And we will risk the ship, ourselves and all.

O my brave soul!
O farther farther sail!
O daring joy, but safe! are they not all the seas of God?
O farther, farther, farther sail!

Good-bye My Fancy!

Good-bye my Fancy!
Farewell dear mate, dear love!
I'm going away, I know not where,
Or to what fortune, or whether I may ever see you again,
So Good-bye my Fancy.

Now for my last—let me look back a moment;
The slower fainter ticking of the clock is in me,
Exit, nightfall, and soon the heart-thud stopping.

Long have we lived, joy'd, caress'd together;
Delightful!—now separation—Good-bye my Fancy.   10

Yet let me not be too hasty,
Long indeed have we lived, slept, filter'd, become really
    blended into one;
Then if we die we die together, (yes, we'll remain one,)
If we go anywhere we'll go together to meet what happens,
May-be we'll be better off and blither, and learn
    something,
May-be it is yourself now really ushering me to the true
    songs, (who knows?)
May-be it is you the mortal knob really undoing, turning
    —so now finally,
Good-bye—and hail! my Fancy.

First published in *Good-bye My Fancy*

Preface to the 1855 edition of Leaves of Grass

America does not repel the past or what it has produced under its forms or amid other politics or the idea of castes or the old religions . . . . accepts the lesson with calmness . . . is not so impatient as has been supposed that the slough still sticks to opinions and manners and literature while the life which served its requirements has passed into the new life of the new forms . . . perceives that the corpse is slowly borne from the eating and sleeping rooms of the house . . . perceives that it waits a little while in the door . . . that it was fittest for its days . . . that its action has descended to the stalwart and well-shaped heir who approaches . . . and that he shall be fittest for his days.

The Americans of all nations at any time upon the earth have probably the fullest poetical nature. The United States themselves are essentially the greatest poem. In the history of the earth hitherto the largest and most stirring appear tame and orderly to their ampler largeness and stir. Here at last is something in the doings of man that corresponds with the broadcast doings of the day and night. Here is not merely a nation but a teeming nation of nations. Here is action united from strings necessarily blind to particulars and details magnificently moving in vast masses. Here is the hospitality which forever indicates heroes . . . . Here are the roughs and beards and space and ruggedness and nonchalance that the soul loves. Here the performance disdaining the trivial unapproached in the tremendous audacity of its crowds and groupings and the push of its perspective spreads with crampless and flow-

Preface to the 1855 edition 151

ing breadth and showers its prolific and splendid extravagance. One sees it must indeed own the riches of the summer and winter, and need never be bankrupt while corn grows from the ground or the orchards drop apples or the bays contain fish or men beget children upon women.

Other states indicate themselves in their deputies . . . . but the genius of the United States is not best or most in its executives or legislatures, nor in its ambassadors or authors or colleges or churches or parlors, nor even in its newspapers or inventors . . . but always most in the common people. Their manners speech dress friendship—the freshness and candor of their physiognomy—the picturesque looseness of their carriage . . . their deathless attachment to freedom—their aversion to anything indecorous or soft or mean—the practical acknowledgment of the citizens of one state by the citizens of all other states—the fierceness of their roused resentment—their curiosity and welcome of novelty—their self-esteem and wonderful sympathy—their susceptibility to a slight—the air they have of persons who never knew how it felt to stand in the presence of superiors—the fluency of their speech—their delight in music, the sure symptom of manly tenderness and native elegance of soul . . . their good temper and openhandedness—the terrible significance of their elections—the President's taking off his hat to them not they to him—these too are unrhymed poetry. It awaits the gigantic and generous treatment worthy of it.

The largeness of nature or the nation were monstrous without a corresponding largeness and generosity of the spirit of the citizen. Not nature nor swarming states nor streets and steamships nor prosperous business nor farms nor capital nor learning may suffice for the ideal of man . . . nor suffice the poet. No reminiscences may suffice either. A live nation can always cut a deep mark and can have the best authority the cheapest . . . namely from its own soul. This is the sum of the profitable uses of individuals or states and of present action and grandeur and of the subjects of poets.—As if it were necessary to trot back generation after generation to the eastern records! As if the beauty and sacredness of the demonstrable must fall behind that of the mythical! As if men do not make their mark out of any times! As if the opening of the western continent by discovery and what has transpired since in North and South America were less than the small theatre of the antique or the aimless sleepwalking of the middle ages! The pride of the United States leaves the wealth and finesse of the cities and all returns of commerce and agriculture and all the magnitude of geography or shows of exterior victory to enjoy the breed of fullsized men or one fullsized man unconquerable and simple.

The American poets are to enclose old and new for America is the race of races. Of them a bard is to be commensurate with a people. To him the other continents arrive as contributions . . . he gives them reception for their sake and his own sake. His spirit responds to his country's spirit . . . . he incarnates its geography and natural life and rivers and lakes. Mississippi with annual freshets and changing chutes, Missouri and Columbia and Ohio and Saint Lawrence with the falls and beautiful masculine Hudson, do not embouchure where they spend themselves more than they embouchure into him. The blue breadth over the inland sea of Virginia and Maryland and the sea off Massachusetts and Maine and over Manhattan bay and over Champlain and Erie and over Ontario and Huron and Michigan and Superior, and over the Texan and Mexican and Floridian and Cuban seas and over the seas off California and Oregon, is not tallied by the blue breadth of the waters below more than the breadth of above and below is tallied by him. When the long Atlantic coast stretches longer and the Pacific coast stretches longer he easily stretches with them north or south. He spans between them also from east to west and reflects what is between them. On him rise solid growths that offset the growths of pine and cedar and hemlock and liveoak and locust and chestnut and cypress and hickory and limetree and cottonwood and tuliptree and cactus and wildvine and tamarind and persimmon . . . . and tangles as tangled as any canebrake or swamp . . . . and forests coated with transparent ice and icicles hanging from the boughs and crackling in the wind . . . . and sides and peaks of mountains . . . . and pasturage sweet and free as savannah or upland or prairie . . . . with flights and songs and screams that answer those of the wildpigeon and highhold and orchard-oriole and coot and surf-duck

Preface to the 1855 edition 153

and redshouldered-hawk and fish-hawk and white-ibis and indian-hen and cat-owl and water-pheasant and qua-bird and pied-sheldrake and blackbird and mockingbird and buzzard and condor and night-heron and eagle. To him the hereditary countenance descends both mother's and father's. To him enter the essences of the real things and past and present events—of the enormous diversity of temperature and agriculture and mines—the tribes of red aborigines—the weatherbeaten vessels entering new ports or making landings on rocky coasts—the first settlements north or south—the rapid stature and muscle—the haughty defiance of '76, and the war and peace and formation of the constitution . . . . the union always surrounded by blatherers and always calm and impregnable —the perpetual coming of immigrants—the wharfhem'd cities and superior marine—the unsurveyed interior—the loghouses and clearings and wild animals and hunters and trappers . . . . the free commerce—the fisheries and whaling and gold-digging—the endless gestation of new states—the convening of Congress every December, the members duly coming up from all climates and the uttermost parts . . . . the noble character of the young mechanics and of all free American workmen and workwomen. . . . the general ardor and friendliness and enterprise—the perfect equality of the female with the male . . . . the large amativeness—the fluid movement of the population—the factories and mercantile life and labor-saving machinery—the Yankee swap—the New-York firemen and the target excursion—the southern plantation life—the character of the northeast and of the northwest and southwest—slavery and the tremulous spreading of hands to protect it, and the stern opposition to it which shall never cease till it ceases or the speaking of tongues and the moving of lips cease. For such the expression of the American poet is to be transcendant and new. It is to be indirect and not direct or descriptive or epic. Its quality goes through these to much more. Let the age and wars of other nations be chanted and their eras and characters be illustrated and that finish the verse. Not so the great psalm of the republic. Here the theme is creative and has vista. Here comes one among the wellbeloved stonecutters and plans with decision and science and sees the solid and beautiful forms of the future where there are now no solid forms.

Of all nations the United States with veins full of poetical stuff most need poets and will doubtless have the greatest and use them the greatest. Their Presidents shall not be their common referee so much as their poets shall. Of all mankind the great poet is the equable man. Not in him but off from him things are grotesque or eccentric or fail of their sanity. Nothing out of its place is good and nothing in its place is bad. He bestows on every object or quality its fit proportions neither more nor less. He is the arbiter of the diverse and he is the key. He is the equalizer of his age and land . . . . he supplies what wants supplying and checks what wants checking. If peace is the routine out of him speaks the spirit of peace, large, rich, thrifty, building vast and populous cities, encouraging agriculture and the arts and commerce—lighting the study of man, the soul, immortality—federal, state or municipal government, marriage, health, freetrade, intertravel by land and sea . . . . nothing too close, nothing too far off . . . the stars not too far off. In war he is the most deadly force of the war. Who recruits him recruits horse and foot . . . he fetches parks of artillery the best that engineer ever knew. If the time becomes slothful and heavy he knows how to arouse it . . . he can make every word he speaks draw blood. Whatever stagnates in the flat of custom or obedience or legislation he never stagnates. Obedience does not master him, he masters it. High up out of reach he stands turning a concentrated light . . . he turns the pivot with his finger . . . he baffles the swiftest runners as he stands and easily overtakes and envelops them. The time straying toward infidelity and confections and persiflage he withholds by his steady faith . . . he spreads out his dishes . . . he offers the sweet firmfibred meat that grows men and women. His brain is the ultimate brain. He is no arguer . . . he is judgment. He judges not as the judge judges but as the sun falling around a helpless thing. As he sees the farthest he has the most faith. His thoughts are the hymns of the praise of things. In the talk on the soul and eternity and God off of his equal plane he is silent. He sees eternity less like a play with a prologue and denouement . . . . he sees eternity in men and women . . . he does not see men and women as dreams or dots. Faith is the antiseptic of the soul . . . it pervades the common people and preserves them . . . they never give up believing and expecting and trusting. There is that indescribable freshness and unconsciousness about an illiterate person that humbles and mocks the power of the noblest expressive genius. The poet sees for a certainty how one not a great artist may be just as sacred and perfect as the greatest artist. . . . . . The power to destroy or remould is freely used by him but never the power of attack. What is past is past. If he does not expose superior models and prove himself by every step he takes he is not what is wanted. The presence of the greatest poet conquers . . . not parleying or struggling or any prepared attempts. Now he has passed that way see after him! there is not left any vestige of despair or misanthropy or cunning or exclusiveness or the ignominy of a nativity or color or delusion of hell or the necessity of hell . . . . . and no man thenceforward shall be degraded for ignorance or weakness or sin.

The greatest poet hardly knows pettiness or triviality. If he breathes into any thing that was before thought small it dilates with the grandeur and life of the universe. He is a seer . . . . he is individual . . . he is complete in himself . . . . the others are as good as he, only he sees it and they do not. He is not one of the chorus . . . . he does not stop for any regulations . . . he is the president of regulation. What the eyesight does to the rest he does to the rest. Who knows the curious mystery of the eyesight? The other senses corroborate themselves, but this is removed from any proof but its own and foreruns the identities of the spiritual world. A single glance of it mocks all the investigations of man and all the instruments and books of the earth and all reasoning. What is marvellous? what is unlikely? what is impossible or baseless or vague? after you have once just opened the space of a peachpit and given audience to far and near and to the sunset and had all things enter with electric swiftness softly and duly without confusion or jostling or jam.

The land and sea, the animals fishes and birds, the sky of heaven and the orbs, the forests mountains and rivers, are not small themes . . . but folks expect of the poet to indicate more than the beauty and dignity which always attach to dumb real objects . . . . they expect him to indicate the path between reality and their souls. Men and women perceive the beauty well enough . . probably as well as he. The passionate tenacity of hunters, woodmen, early risers, cultivators of gardens and orchards and fields, the love of healthy women for the manly form, seafaring persons, drivers of horses, the passion for light and the open air, all is an old varied sign of the unfailing perception of beauty and of a residence of the poetic in outdoor people. They can never be assisted by poets to perceive . . . some may but they never can. The poetic quality is not marshalled in rhyme or uniformity or abstract addresses to things nor in melancholy complaints or good precepts, but is the life of these and much else and is in the soul. The profit of rhyme is that it drops seeds of a sweeter and more luxuriant rhyme, and of uniformity that it conveys itself into its own roots in the ground out of sight. The rhyme and uniformity of perfect poems show the free growth of metrical laws and bud from them as unerringly and loosely as lilacs or roses on a bush, and take shapes as compact as the shapes of chestnuts and oranges and melons and pears, and shed the perfume impalpable to form. The fluency and ornaments of the finest poems or music or orations or recitations are not independent but dependent. All beauty comes from beautiful blood and a beautiful brain. If the greatnesses are in conjunction in a man or woman it is enough . . . . the fact will prevail through the universe . . . . but the gaggery and gilt of a million years will not prevail. Who troubles himself about his ornaments or fluency is lost. This is what you shall do: Love the earth and sun and the animals, despise riches, give alms to every one that asks, stand up for the stupid and crazy, devote your income and labor to others, hate tyrants, argue not concerning God, have patience and indulgence toward the people, take off your hat to nothing known or unknown or to any man or number of men, go freely with powerful uneducated persons and with the young and with the mothers of families, read these leaves in the open air every season of every year of your life, re-examine all you have been told at school or church or in any book, dismiss whatever insults your own soul, and your very flesh shall be a great poem and have the richest fluency not only in its words but in the silent lines of its lips and face and between the lashes of your eyes and in every motion and joint of your body. . . . . The poet shall not spend his time in unneeded work. He shall know that the ground is always ready ploughed and manured . . . . others may not know it but he shall. He shall go directly to the creation. His trust shall master the trust of everything he touches . . . . and shall master all attachment.

The known universe has one complete lover and that is the greatest poet. He consumes an eternal passion and is indifferent which chance happens and which possible contingency of fortune or misfortune and persuades daily and hourly his delicious pay. What balks or breaks others is fuel for his burning progress to contact and amorous joy. Other proportions of the reception of pleasure dwindle to nothing to his proportions. All expected from heaven or from the highest he is rapport with in the sight of the daybreak or a scene of the winter woods or the presence of children playing or with his arm round the neck of a man or woman. His love above all love has leisure and expanse . . . . he leaves room ahead of himself. He is no irresolute or suspicious lover . . . he is sure . . . he scorns intervals. His experience and the showers and thrills are not for nothing. Nothing can jar him . . . . suffering and darkness cannot—death and fear cannot. To him complaint and jealousy and envy are corpses buried and rotten in the earth . . . . he saw them buried. The sea is not surer of the shore or the shore of the sea than he is of the fruition of his love and of all perfection and beauty.

The fruition of beauty is no chance of hit or miss . . . it is inevitable as life . . . . it is exact and plumb as gravitation. From the eyesight proceeds another eyesight and from the hearing proceeds another hearing and from the voice proceeds another voice eternally curious of the harmony of things with man. To these respond perfections not only in the committees that were supposed to stand for the rest but in the rest themselves just the same. These understand the law of perfection in masses and floods . . . that its finish is to each for itself and onward from itself

... that it is profuse and impartial ... that there is not a minute of the light or dark nor an acre of the earth or sea without it—nor any direction of the sky nor any trade or employment nor any turn of events. This is the reason that about the proper expression of beauty there is precision and balance ... one part does not need to be thrust above another. The best singer is not the one who has the most lithe and powerful organ ... the pleasure of poems is not in them that take the handsomest measure and similes and sound.

Without effort and without exposing in the least how it is done the greatest poet brings the spirit of any or all events and passions and scenes and persons some more and some less to bear on your individual character as you hear or read. To do this well is to compete with the laws that pursue and follow time. What is the purpose must surely be there and the clue of it must be there .... and the faintest indication is the indication of the best and then becomes the clearest indication. Past and present and future are not disjoined but joined. The greatest poet forms the consistence of what is to be from what has been and is. He drags the dead out of their coffins and stands them again on their feet .... he says to the past, Rise and walk before me that I may realize you. He learns the lesson .... he places himself where the future becomes present. The greatest poet does not only dazzle his rays over character and scenes and passions ... he finally ascends and finishes all ... he exhibits the pinnacles that no man can tell what they are for or what is beyond .... he glows a moment on the extremest verge. He is most wonderful in his last half-hidden smile or frown ... by that flash of the moment of parting the one that sees it shall be encouraged or terrified afterwards for many years. The greatest poet does not moralize or make applications of morals ... he knows the soul. The soul has that measureless pride which consists in never acknowledging any lessons but its own. But it has sympathy as measureless as its pride and the one balances the other and neither can stretch too far while it stretches in company with the other. The inmost secrets of art sleep with the twain. The greatest poet has lain close betwixt both and they are vital in his style and thoughts.

The art of art, the glory of expression and the sunshine of the light of letters is simplicity. Nothing is better than simplicity . . . . nothing can make up for excess or for the lack of definiteness. To carry on the heave of impulse and pierce intellectual depths and give all subjects their articulations are powers neither common nor very uncommon. But to speak in literature with the perfect rectitude and insousiance of the movements of animals and the unimpeachableness of the sentiment of trees in the woods and grass by the roadside is the flawless triumph of art. If you have looked on him who has achieved it you have looked on one of the masters of the artists of all nations and times. You shall not contemplate the flight of the graygull over the bay or the mettlesome action of the blood horse or the tall leaning of sunflowers on their stalk or the appearance of the sun journeying through heaven or the appearance of the moon afterward with any more satisfaction than you shall contemplate him. The greatest poet has less a marked style and is more the channel of thoughts and things without increase or diminution, and is the free channel of himself. He swears to his art, I will not be meddlesome, I will not have in my writing any elegance or effect or originality to hang in the way between me and the rest like curtains. I will have nothing hang in the way, not the richest curtains. What I tell I tell for precisely what it is. Let who may exalt or startle or fascinate or sooth I will have purposes as health or heat or snow has and be as regardless of observation. What I experience or portray shall go from my composition without a shred of my composition. You shall stand by my side and look in the mirror with me.

The old red blood and stainless gentility of great poets will be proved by their unconstraint. A heroic person walks at his ease through and out of that custom or precedent or authority that suits him not. Of the traits of the brotherhood of writers savans musicians inventors and artists nothing is finer than silent defiance advancing from new free forms. In the need of poems philosophy politics mechanism science behaviour, the craft of art, an appropriate native grand-opera, shipcraft, or any craft, he is greatest forever and forever who contributes the greatest original practical example. The cleanest expression is that which finds no sphere worthy of itself and makes one.

The messages of great poets to each man and woman are, Come to us on equal terms, Only then can you understand us, We are no better than you, What we enclose you enclose, What we enjoy you may enjoy. Did you suppose there could be only one Supreme? We affirm there can be unnumbered Supremes, and that one does not countervail another any more than one eyesight countervails another . . and that men can be good or grand only of the consciousness of their supremacy within them. What do you think is the grandeur of storms and dismemberments and the deadliest battles and wrecks and the wildest fury of the elements and the power of the sea and the motion of nature and of the throes of human desires and dignity and hate and love? It is that something in the soul which says, Rage on, Whirl on, I tread master here and everywhere, Master of the spasms of the sky and of the shatter of the sea, Master of nature and passion and death, And of all terror and all pain.

The American bards shall be marked for generosity and affection and for encouraging competitors . . They shall be kosmos . . without monopoly or secresy . . glad to pass any thing to any one . . hungry for equals night and day. They shall not be careful of riches and privilege . . . . they shall be riches and privilege . . . . they shall perceive who the most affluent man is. The most affluent man is he that confronts all the shows he sees by equivalents out of the stronger wealth of himself. The American bard shall delineate no class of persons nor one or two out of the strata of interests nor love most nor truth most nor the soul most nor the body most . . . . and not be for the eastern states more than the western or the northern states more than the southern.

Exact science and its practical movements are no checks on the greatest poet but always his encouragement and support. The outset and remembrance are there . . there the arms that lifted him first and brace him best . . . . there he returns after all his goings and comings. The sailor and traveler . . the anatomist chemist astronomer geologist phrenologist spiritualist mathematician historian and lexicographer are not poets, but they are the lawgivers of poets and their construction underlies the structure of every perfect poem. No matter what rises or is uttered they sent the seed of the conception of it . . . of them and by them stand the visible proofs of souls . . . . . always of their fatherstuff must be begotten the sinewy races of bards. If there shall be love and content between the father and the son and if the greatness of the son is the exuding of the greatness of the father there shall be love between the poet and the man of demonstrable science. In the beauty of poems are the tuft and final applause of science.

Great is the faith of the flush of knowledge and of the investigation of the depths of qualities and things. Cleaving and circling here swells the soul of the poet yet it president of itself always. The depths are fathomless and therefore calm. The innocence and nakedness are resumed . . . they are neither modest nor immodest. The whole theory of the special and supernatural and all that was twined with it or educed out of it departs as a dream. What has ever happened . . . . what happens and whatever may or shall happen, the vital laws enclose all . . . . they are sufficient for any case and for all cases . . . none to be hurried or retarded . . . . any miracle of affairs or persons inadmissible in the vast clear scheme where every motion and every spear of grass and the frames and spirits of men and women and all that concerns them are unspeakably perfect miracles all referring to all and each distinct and in its place. It is also not consistent with the reality of the soul to admit that there is anything in the known universe more divine than men and women.

Men and women and the earth and all upon it are simply to be taken as they are, and the investigation of their past and present and future shall be unintermitted and shall be done with perfect candor. Upon this basis philosophy speculates ever looking toward the poet, ever regarding the eternal tendencies of all toward happiness never inconsistent with what is clear to the senses and to the soul. For the eternal tendencies of all toward happiness make the only point of sane philosophy. Whatever comprehends less than that . . . whatever is less than the laws of light and of astronomical motion . . . or less than the laws that follow the thief the liar the glutton and the

drunkard through this life and doubtless afterward
. . . . . or less than vast stretches of time or the slow
formation of density or the patient upheaving of strata—
is of no account. Whatever would put God in a poem or
system of philosophy as contending against some being or
influence is also of no account. Sanity and ensemble characterise the great master . . . spoilt in one principle all is
spoilt. The great master has nothing to do with miracles.
He sees health for himself in being one of the mass . . . .
he sees the hiatus in singular eminence. To the perfect
shape comes common ground. To be under the general law
is great for that is to correspond with it. The master knows
that he is unspeakably great and that all are unspeakably
great . . . . that nothing for instance is greater than to
conceive children and bring them up well . . . that to be
is just as great as to perceive or tell.

In the make of the great masters the idea of political
liberty is indispensable. Liberty takes the adherence of heroes wherever men and women exist . . . . but never
takes any adherence or welcome from the rest more than
from poets. They are the voice and exposition of liberty.
They out of ages are worthy the grand idea . . . . to
them it is confided and they must sustain it. Nothing has
precedence of it and nothing can warp or degrade it. The
attitude of great poets is to cheer up slaves and horrify
despots. The turn of their necks, the sound of their feet,
the motions of their wrists, are full of hazard to the one
and hope to the other. Come nigh them awhile and
though they neither speak or advise you shall learn the
faithful American lesson. Liberty is poorly served by men
whose good intent is quelled from one failure or two failures or any number of failures, or from the casual indifference or ingratitude of the people, or from the sharp show
of the tushes of power, or the bringing to bear soldiers and
cannon or any penal statutes. Liberty relies upon itself, invites no one, promises nothing, sits in calmness and light,
is positive and composed, and knows no discouragement.
The battle rages with many a loud alarm and frequent advance and retreat . . . . the enemy triumphs . . . . the
prison, the handcuffs, the iron necklace and anklet, the
scaffold, garrote and leadballs do their work . . . . the
cause is asleep . . . . the strong throats are choked with

Preface to the 1855 edition 163

their own blood . . . . the young men drop their eyelashes toward the ground when they pass each other . . . . and is liberty gone out of that place? No never. When liberty goes it is not the first to go nor the second or third to go . . it waits for all the rest to go . . it is the last . . . When the memories of the old martyrs are faded utterly away . . . . when the large names of patriots are laughed at in the public halls from the lips of the orators . . . . when the boys are no more christened after the same but christened after tyrants and traitors instead . . . . when the laws of the free are grudgingly permitted and laws for informers and bloodmoney are sweet to the taste of the people . . . . when I and you walk abroad upon the earth stung with compassion at the sight of numberless brothers answering our equal friendship and calling no man master —and when we are elated with noble joy at the sight of slaves . . . . when the soul retires in the cool communion of the night and surveys its experience and has much extasy over the word and deed that put back a helpless innocent person into the gripe of the gripers or into any cruel inferiority . . . . when those in all parts of these states who could easier realize the true American character but do not yet—when the swarms of cringers, suckers, doughfaces, lice of politics, planners of sly involutions for their own preferment to city offices or state legislatures or the judiciary or congress or the presidency, obtain a response of love and natural deference from the people whether they get the offices or no . . . . when it is better to be a bound booby and rogue in office at a high salary than the poorest free mechanic or farmer with his hat unmoved from his head and firm eyes and a candid and generous heart . . . . and when servility by town or state or the federal government or any oppression on a large scale or small scale can be tried on without its own punishment following duly after in exact proportion against the smallest chance of escape . . . . or rather when all life and all the souls of men and women are discharged from any part of the earth—then only shall the instinct of liberty be discharged from that part of the earth.

As the attributes of the poets of the kosmos concentre in the real body and soul and in the pleasure of things they possess the superiority of genuineness over all fiction and romance. As they emit themselves facts are showered over with light . . . . the daylight is lit with more volatile light . . . . also the deep between the setting and rising sun goes deeper many fold. Each precise object or condition or combination or process exhibits a beauty . . . . the multiplication table its—old age its—the carpenter's trade its—the grand-opera its . . . . the hugehulled cleanshaped New-York clipper at sea under steam or full sail gleams with unmatched beauty . . . . the American circles and large harmonies of government gleam with theirs . . . . and the commonest definite intentions and actions with theirs. The poets of the kosmos advance through all interpositions and coverings and turmoils and stratagems to first principles. They are of use . . . . they dissolve poverty from its need and riches from its conceit. You large proprietor they say shall not realize or perceive more than any one else. The owner of the library is not he who holds a legal title to it having bought and paid for it. Any one and every one is owner of the library who can read the same through all the varieties of tongues and subjects and styles, and in whom they enter with ease and take residence and force toward paternity and maternity, and make supple and powerful and rich and large. . . . . These American states strong and healthy and accomplished shall receive no pleasure from violations of natural models and must not permit them. In paintings or mouldings or carvings in mineral or wood, or in the illustrations of books or newspapers, or in any comic or tragic prints, or in the patterns of woven stuffs or any thing to beautify rooms or furniture or costumes, or to put upon cornices or monuments or on the prows or sterns of ships, or to put anywhere before the human eye indoors or out, that which distorts honest shapes or which creates unearthly beings or places or contingencies is a nuisance and revolt. Of the human form especially it is so great it must never be made ridiculous. Of ornaments to a work nothing outre can be allowed . . but those ornaments can be allowed that conform to the perfect facts of the open air and that flow out of the nature of the work and come irrepressibly from it and are necessary to the completion of the work. Most works are most beautiful without ornament. . . Exaggerations will be revenged in human physiology. Clean and vigorous children are jetted and conceived only in those communities where the models of natural forms are public every day. . . . . Great genius and the people of these states must never be demeaned to romances. As soon as histories are properly told there is no more need of romances.

The great poets are also to be known by the absence in them of tricks and by the justification of perfect personal candor. Then folks echo a new cheap joy and a divine voice leaping from their brains: How beautiful is candor! All faults may be forgiven of him who has perfect candor. Henceforth let no man of us lie, for we have seen that openness wins the inner and outer world and that there is no single exception, and that never since our earth gathered itself in a mass have deceit or subterfuge or prevarication attracted its smallest particle or the faintest tinge of a shade—and that through the enveloping wealth and rank of a state or the whole republic of states a sneak or sly person shall be discovered and despised . . . . and that the soul has never been once fooled and never can be fooled . . . . and thrift without the loving nod of the soul is only a fœtid puff . . . . and there never grew up in any of the continents of the globe nor upon any planet or satellite or star, nor upon the asteroids, nor in any part of ethereal space, nor in the midst of density, nor under the fluid wet of the sea, nor in that condition which precedes the birth of babes, nor at any time during the changes of life, nor in that condition that follows what we term death, nor in any stretch of abeyance or action afterward of vitality, nor in any process of formation or reformation anywhere, a being whose instinct hated the truth.

Extreme caution or prudence, the soundest organic health, large hope and comparison and fondness for women and children, large alimentiveness and destructiveness and causality, with a perfect sense of the oneness of nature and the propriety of the same spirit applied to human affairs . . these are called up of the float of the brain of the world to be parts of the greatest poet from his birth out of his mother's womb and from her birth out of her mother's. Caution seldom goes far enough. It has been thought that the prudent citizen was the citizen who applied himself to solid gains and did well for himself and his family and completed a lawful life without debt or crime. The greatest poet sees and admits these economies as he sees the economies of food and sleep, but has higher notions of prudence than to think he gives much when he gives a few slight attentions at the latch of the gate. The premises of the prudence of life are not the hospitality of it or the ripeness and harvest of it. Beyond the independence of a little sum laid aside for burial-money, and of a few clapboards around and shingles overhead on a lot of American soil owned, and the easy dollars that supply the year's plain clothing and meals, the melancholy prudence of the abandonment of such a great being as a man is to the toss and pallor of years of moneymaking with all their scorching days and icy nights and all their stifling deceits and underhanded dodgings, or infinitesimals of parlors, or shameless stuffing while others starve . . and all the loss of the bloom and odor of the earth and of the flowers and atmosphere and of the sea and of the true taste of the women and men you pass or have to do with in youth or middle age, and the issuing sickness and desperate revolt at the close of a life without elevation or naivete, and the ghastly chatter of a death without serenity or majesty, is the great fraud upon modern civilization and forethought, blotching the surface and system which civilization undeniably drafts, and moistening with tears the immense features it spreads and spreads with such velocity before the reached kisses of the soul. . . Still the right explanation remains to be made about prudence. The prudence of the mere wealth and respectability of the most esteemed life appears too faint for the eye to observe at all when little and large alike drop quietly aside at the thought of the prudence suitable for immortality. What is wisdom that fills the thinness of a year or seventy or eighty years to wisdom spaced out by ages and coming back at a certain time with strong reinforcements and rich presents and the clear faces of wedding-guests as far as you can look in every direction running gaily toward you? Only the soul is of itself . . . . all else has reference to what ensues. All that a person does or thinks is of consequence. Not a move can a man or woman make that affects him or her in a day or a month or any part of the direct lifetime or the hour of death but the same affects him or her onward afterward through the indirect lifetime. The indirect is always as great and real as the direct. The spirit receives from the body just as much as it gives to the body. Not one name of word or deed . . not of venereal sores or discolorations . . not the privacy of the onanist . . not of the putrid veins of gluttons or rumdrinkers . . . not peculation or cunning or betrayal or murder . . no serpentine poison of those that seduce women . . not the foolish yielding of women . . not prostitution . . not of any depravity of young men . . not of the attainment of gain by discreditable means . . not any nastiness of appetite . . not any harshness of officers to men or judges to prisoners or fathers to sons or sons to fathers or husbands to wives or bosses to their boys . . not of greedy looks or malignant wishes . . . nor any of the wiles practised by people upon themselves . . . ever is or ever can be stamped on the programme but it is duly realized and returned, and that returned in further performances . . . and they returned again. Nor can the push of charity or personal force ever be any thing else than the profoundest reason, whether it brings arguments to hand or no. No specification is necessary . . to add or subtract or divide is in vain. Little or big, learned or unlearned, white or black, legal or illegal, sick or well, from the first inspiration down the windpipe to the last expiration out of it, all that a male or female does that is vigorous and benevolent and clean is so much sure profit to him or her in the unshakable order of the universe and through the whole scope of it forever. If the savage or felon is wise it is well . . . . if the greatest poet or savan is wise it is simply the same . . if the President or chief justice is wise it is the same . . . if the young mechanic or farmer is wise it is no more or less . . if the prostitute is wise it is no more nor less. The interest will come round . . all will come round. All the best actions of war and peace . . . all help given to relatives and strangers and the poor and old and sorrowful and young children and widows and the sick, and to all shunned persons . . all furtherance of fugitives and of the escape of slaves . . all the self-denial that stood steady and aloof on wrecks and saw others take the seats of the boats . . . all offering of substance or life for the good old cause, or for a friend's sake or opinion's sake . . . all pains of enthusiasts scoffed at by their neighbors . . all the vast sweet love and precious suffering of mothers . . . all honest men baffled in strifes recorded or unrecorded . . . . all the grandeur and good of the few ancient nations whose fragments of annals we inherit . . and all the good of the hundreds of far mightier and more ancient nations unknown to us by name or date or location . . . . all that was ever manfully begun, whether it succeeded or not . . . . all that has at any time been well suggested out of the divine heart of man or by the divinity of his mouth or by the shaping of his great hands . . and all that is well thought or done this day on any part of the surface of the globe . . or on any of the wandering stars or fixed stars by those there as we are here . . or that is henceforth to be well thought or done by you whoever you are, or by any one—these singly and wholly inured at their time and inure now and will inure always to the identities from which they sprung or shall spring. . . Did you guess any of them lived only its moment? The world does not so exist . . no parts palpable or impalpable so exist . . . no result exists now without being from its long antecedent result, and that from its antecedent, and so backward without the farthest mentionable spot coming a bit nearer the beginning than any other spot. . . . . Whatever satisfies the soul is truth. The prudence of the greatest poet answers at last the craving and glut of the soul, is not contemptuous of less ways of prudence if they conform to its ways, puts off nothing, permits no let-up for its own case or any case, has no particular sabbath or judgment-day, divides not the living from the dead or the righteous from the unrighteous, is satisfied with the present, matches every thought or act by its correlative, knows no possible forgiveness or deputed atonement . . knows that the young man who composedly periled his life and lost it has done exceeding well for himself, while the man who has not periled his life and retains it to old age in riches and ease has perhaps achieved nothing for himself worth mentioning . . and that only that person has no great prudence to learn who has learnt to prefer real longlived things, and favors body and soul the same, and perceives the indirect assuredly following the direct, and what evil or good he does leaping onward and waiting to meet him again—and who in his

Preface to the 1855 edition 169

spirit in any emergency whatever neither hurries or avoids death.

The direct trial of him who would be the greatest poet is today. If he does not flood himself with the immediate age as with vast oceanic tides . . . . . and if he does not attract his own land body and soul to himself and hang on its neck with incomparable love and plunge his semitic muscle into its merits and demerits . . . and if he be not himself the age transfigured . . . . and if to him is not opened the eternity which gives similitude to all periods and locations and processes and animate and inanimate forms, and which is the bond of time, and rises up from its inconceivable vagueness and infiniteness in the swimming shape of today, and is held by the ductile anchors of life, and makes the present spot the passage from what was to what shall be, and commits itself to the representation of this wave of an hour and this one of the sixty beautiful children of the wave—let him merge in the general run and wait his development. . . . . Still the final test of poems or any character or work remains. The prescient poet projects himself centuries ahead and judges performer or performance after the changes of time. Does it live through them? Does it still hold on untired? Will the same style and the direction of genius to similar points be satisfactory now? Has no new discovery in science or arrival at superior planes of thought and judgment and behaviour fixed him or his so that either can be looked down upon? Have the marches of tens and hundreds and thousands of years made willing detours to the right hand and the left hand for his sake? Is he beloved long and long after he is buried? Does the young man think often of him? and the young woman think often of him? and do the middleaged and the old think of him?

A great poem is for ages and ages in common and for all degrees and complexions and all departments and sects and for a woman as much as a man and a man as much as a woman. A great poem is no finish to a man or woman but rather a beginning. Has any one fancied he could sit at last under some due authority and rest satisfied with explanations and realize and be content and full? To no such terminus does the greatest poet bring . . . he brings neither cessation or sheltered fatness and ease. The touch of him tells in action. Whom he takes he takes with firm sure grasp into live regions previously unattained . . . . thenceforward is no rest . . . . they see the space and ineffable sheen that turn the old spots and lights into dead vacuums. The companion of him beholds the birth and progress of stars and learns one of the meanings. Now there shall be a man cohered out of tumult and chaos . . . . the elder encourages the younger and shows him how . . . they two shall launch off fearlessly together till the new world fits an orbit for itself and looks unabashed on the lesser orbits of the stars and sweeps through the ceaseless rings and shall never be quiet again.

There will soon be no more priests. Their work is done. They may wait awhile . . perhaps a generation or two . . dropping off by degrees. A superior breed shall take their place. . . . the gangs of kosmos and prophets en masse shall take their place. A new order shall arise and they shall be the priests of man, and every man shall be his own priest. The churches built under their umbrage shall be the churches of men and women. Through the divinity of themselves shall the kosmos and the new breed of poets be interpreters of men and women and of all events and things. They shall find their inspiration in real objects today, symptoms of the past and future . . . . They shall not deign to defend immortality or God or the perfection of things or liberty or the exquisite beauty and reality of the soul. They shall arise in America and be responded to from the remainder of the earth.

The English language befriends the grand American expression . . . . it is brawny enough and limber and full enough. On the tough stock of a race who through all change of circumstances was never without the idea of political liberty, which is the animus of all liberty, it has attracted the terms of daintier and gayer and subtler and more elegant tongues. It is the powerful language of resistance . . . it is the dialect of common sense. It is the speech of the proud and melancholy races and of all who aspire. It is the chosen tongue to express growth faith self-esteem freedom justice equality friendliness amplitude prudence decision and courage. It is the medium that shall well nigh express the inexpressible.

No great literature nor any like style of behaviour or

Preface to the 1855 edition 171

oratory or social intercourse or household arrangements or public institutions or the treatment by bosses of employed people, nor executive detail or detail of the army or navy, nor spirit of legislation or courts or police or tuition or architecture or songs or amusements or the costumes of young men, can long elude the jealous and passionate instinct of American standards. Whether or no the sign appears from the mouths of the people, it throbs a live interrogation in every freeman's and freewoman's heart after that which passes by or this built to remain. Is it uniform with my country? Are its disposals without ignominious distinctions? Is it for the evergrowing communes of brothers and lovers, large, well-united, proud beyond the old models, generous beyond all models? Is it something grown fresh out of the fields or drawn from the sea for use to me today here? I know that what answers for me an American must answer for any individual or nation that serves for a part of my materials. Does this answer? or is it without reference to universal needs? or sprung of the needs of the less developed society of special ranks? or old needs of pleasure overlaid by modern science and forms? Does this acknowledge liberty with audible and absolute acknowledgement, and set slavery at nought for life and death? Will it help breed one goodshaped and wellhung man, and a woman to be his perfect and independent mate? Does it improve manners? Is it for the nursing of the young of the republic? Does it solve readily with the sweet milk of the nipples of the breasts of the mother of many children? Has it too the old ever-fresh forbearance and impartiality? Does it look with the same love on the last born and on those hardening toward stature, and on the errant, and on those who disdain all strength of assault outside of their own?

The poems distilled from other poems will probably pass away. The coward will surely pass away. The expectation of the vital and great can only be satisfied by the demeanor of the vital and great.

The swarms of the polished deprecating and reflectors and the polite float off and leave no remembrance. America prepares with composure and goodwill for the visitors that have sent word. It is not intellect that is to be their warrant and welcome. The talented, the artist, the ingenious, the editor, the statesman, the erudite . . they are not unappreciated . . they fall in their place and do their work. The soul of the nation also does its work. No disguise can pass on it . . no disguise can conceal from it. It rejects none, it permits all. Only toward as good as itself and toward the like of itself will it advance half-way. An individual is as superb as a nation when he has the qualities which make a superb nation. The soul of the largest and wealthiest and proudest nation may well go half-way to meet that of its poets. The signs are effectual. There is no fear of mistake. If the one is true the other is true. The proof of a poet is that his country absorbs him as affectionately as he has absorbed it.

bibliography

writings

The Collected Writings of Walt Whitman, general eds. Gay Wilson Allen and Sculley Bradley, 16 vols. (New York, 1961–   ). This scholarly edition will supersede *The Complete Writings of Walt Whitman,* eds. R. M. Bucke, T. B. Harned, and H. L. Traubel, 10 vols. (New York, 1902).
The Uncollected Poetry and Prose of Walt Whitman, ed. Emory Holloway, 2 vols. (New York, 1921).

biography and criticism

Allen, Gay Wilson, *The Solitary Singer: A Critical Biography of Walt Whitman* (New York, 1955). The standard biography.
———, *Walt Whitman Handbook* (New York, 1946).
Chase, Richard, *Walt Whitman Reconsidered* (New York, 1955).
Miller, Edwin Haviland, *Walt Whitman's Poetry: A Psychological Journey* (Boston, 1968).
Miller, James E., Jr., *A Critical Guide to Leaves of Grass* (Chicago, 1957).
Traubel, Horace L., *With Walt Whitman in Camden,* 5 vols. (New York and Carbondale, Ill., 1906–1964).

Significant essays on Whitman are those by D. H. Lawrence (*Studies in Classic American Literature,* 1923), F. O. Matthiessen (*American Renaissance: Art and Expression in the Age of Emerson and Whitman,* 1941), Leo Spitzer (*Essays on English and American Literature,* 1962, which reprints Spitzer's essay written in 1949), Malcolm Cowley (*Walt Whitman's Leaves of Grass—*

The First [1855] Edition, 1959); Kenneth Burke (*Leaves of Grass One Hundred Years After*, ed. Milton Hindus, 1955), Willard Thorp (*Eight American Authors*, ed. Floyd Stovall, 1956), and Roy Harvey Pearce (*The Continuity of American Poetry*, 1961). Many of these essays appear in *A Century of Whitman Criticism*, ed. Edwin Haviland Miller (Bloomington, Ind., 1969).

Other essays appear in *The Presence of Walt Whitman*, ed. R. W. B. Lewis (New York, 1962), in *Whitman: A Collection of Critical Essays*, ed. Roy Harvey Pearce (Englewood Cliffs, N.J., 1962), and in *The Artistic Legacy of Walt Whitman: Essays in Honor of Gay Wilson Allen*, ed. Edwin Haviland Miller (New York, 1969). For Bibliography, consult *Literary History of the United States* (New York, 1962), 759–768, and *Supplement*, 203–207.